INTRODUCTION

Welcome to the world of digital publishing ~ the book you now hold in your hand, while unchanged from the original **1967** edition, was printed using the latest state of the art digital technology. The advent of print-on-demand has forever changed the publishing process, never has information been so accessible and it is our hope that this book serves your informational needs for years to come. If this is your first exposure to digital publishing, we hope that you are pleased with the results. Many more titles of interest to the classic automobile and motorcycle enthusiast, collector and restorer are available via our website at **www.VelocePress.com.** We hope that you find this title as interesting as we do.

NOTE FROM THE PUBLISHER

The information presented is true and complete to the best of our knowledge. All recommendations are made without any guarantees on the part of the author or the publisher, who also disclaim all liability incurred with the use of this information.

TRADEMARKS

We recognize that some words, model names and designations, for example, mentioned herein are the property of the trademark holder. We use them for identification purposes only. This is not an official publication.

INFORMATION ON THE USE OF THIS PUBLICATION

This manual is an invaluable resource for the classic **Honda** enthusiast and a "must have" for owners interested in performing their own maintenance. However, in today's information age we are constantly subject to changes in common practice, new technology, availability of improved materials and increased awareness of chemical toxicity. As such, it is advised that the user consult with an experienced professional prior to undertaking any procedure described herein. While every care has been taken to ensure correctness of information, it is obviously not possible to guarantee complete freedom from errors or omissions or to accept liability arising from such errors or omissions. Therefore, any individual that uses the information contained within, or elects to perform or participate in do-it-yourself repairs or modifications acknowledges that there is a risk factor involved and that the publisher or its associates cannot be held responsible for personal injury or property damage resulting from the use of the information or the outcome of such procedures.

It is important that the reader recognizes that any instructions may refer to either the right-hand or left-hand sides of the vehicle or the components and that the directions are followed carefully. One final word of advice, this publication is intended to be used as a reference guide, and when in doubt the reader should consult with a qualified technician.

The Book of the
HONDA

BY

JOHN THORPE

Published in 1967 by
FLOYD CLYMER PUBLICATIONS
World's Largest Publisher of Books Relating to
Automobile, Motorcycles, Motor Racing, and Americana
222 NO. VIRGIL AVENUE, LOS ANGELES 4, CALIFORNIA

ANNOUNCEMENT

This Book of the Honda was first published in England by famous authority/author John Thorpe. The models listed on the cover are well covered for a low-priced book. They are the popular ones built through 1964 and, in many instances, there have been no basic changes; therefore the book covers many of the later models. We also have service manuals and handbooks covering individual models.

The book is not a shop manual, nor is it intended to make every Honda owner an expert mechanic. We suggest that, for important repair work, the owner go to his dealer for proper servicing. The authorized Honda dealer has mechanics trained in Honda factory service methods, the necessary special tools and genuine Honda parts.

Inasmuch as the book was written and published in England there are many special accessories, parts and components not available in the U.S. Rather than eliminate description of this special equipment we have published the book exactly as written — so tires are tyres, color is colour, and spark plugs are sparking plugs. Could anything be more unusual than a book written by an Englishman about a Japanese cycle and published by a Yankee?

So cheerio, sayonara and so long — we hope you enjoy this book.

Floyd Clymer

FOREWORD

It is always a pleasure to me to see some fresh mark of the high esteem in which Honda products are held. Each is a tribute not only to those who have designed the machines and directed the policy of the now world-wide Honda organization, but also to the enthusiasm and skill of our conscientious workers in all parts of Europe and Asia. For we are enthusiasts too.

That a technical journalist of John Thorpe's standing has produced a book for British readers so soon after Honda's establishment in Europe is particularly gratifying. For an overseas manufacturer, Britain is a market notorious for accepting only the best in design and workmanship. Thus John Thorpe's book reflects not just a commercial success but—just as important to us—the fact that Honda riders cherish their machines.

I can commend it to them as a useful ready-reference volume which will certainly help them to keep their Hondas in trim for the many thousands of miles of carefree riding which I hope—and know—they will enjoy.

I. NEUCHI

(Director, European Honda Motor Trading, G.m.b.H.)

PREFACE

IN March 1959 I was one of a crowd of European motoring journalists who were gathered round a modest stand at the Amsterdam Show to look at a rarity—the first Japanese motor-cycle ever to be imported into Europe! At that time Japan—so far as its motor-cycle manufacturers had any reputation at all—was renowned mainly for making underpowered machines which were composite copies of various European designs.

This machine was different—though to our eyes it looked ungainly. It was a blue-painted 250 c.c. parallel twin. Its pressed-steel forks, its tank, even its headlamp and spring units were squarish in appearance. It had an electric starter tacked on at the front—a system which even the Italians had never succeeded in turning into a practical proposition. And nobody could remember ever hearing of the name it bore—Honda.

How little did we know then that we were being privileged to have an early glance at a range of machines which were soon to join the elect few—Scott, Velocette, Vincent, Norton, Brough, B.M.W., and one or two others—which can excite in their owners a loyalty so deep and so fanatical that no other mount is good enough for them.

Within a few years the Honda had become one of this band. Its overhead camshaft power unit, in 125 c.c. and 250 c.c. form, proved to be so basically sound in design and so well engineered that engine speeds which a few years before might have been associated with gas turbines suddenly became normal for everyday machines. Yet, for all that, there was no loss of flexibility—my own 1962 C.92 tourer proved itself to be capable of a rev-range of something like 7,500 r.p.m. in top gear; and its sporting CB.72 successor had a usable range of around 6,000 r.p.m. in top.

Racing successes, of course, helped to bring the Honda name before the public. Then came another breakthrough—the introduction of the 50 c.c. range of motor-cycles and scooterettes. In Britain, this was marked by a non-stop seven-day run by three of these tiny machines, at Goodwood, the Sussex motor-racing circuit. Officially observed by the Auto-Cycle Union (the controlling body of motor-cycle sport in Britain) a C.110D motor-cycle covered 5,897 miles; a C.102 covered 4,935 miles; and a C.100 covered 5,023 miles. The best fuel consumption for the distance bettered 140 m.p.g. and worst 124 m.p.g. The motor-cycle had averaged 35 m.p.h. and the scooterettes only slightly under 30 m.p.h. This won Honda the Maudes Trophy.

Round about this time I was myself conducting a 2,200 miles Press test of a C.100, with permission from the U.K. Branch of European Honda to break it if I could. Despite the hardest driving I could devise, and

PREFACE

despite deliberate neglect of even such essentials as oil top-ups and battery checks, the machine not only failed to blow up but also beat all my personal point-to-point and hill-climbing performances for a "50" on test routes I had used for about 200 various models for several moped and scooter magazines.

Such treatment—though good for a story—is not one which I would recommend to the private owner. Hence this book, in the preparation of which I have been admirably assisted by the enthusiastic staff of European Honda's U.K. Branch. It is designed to enable the newcomer to the Honda camp, and to motor-cycling, to service his own machine and to keep it in a tip-top running order. For his benefit, I have included much basic data. But the old hand, like myself, has not been forgotten—the specialized chapters contain enough information to permit an experienced motor-cyclist to strip and rebuild a machine if need be. From my own experience of Hondas I would say that till a very considerable mileage has been covered that is something you will only have to do for fun. And I have owned 50, 125 and 250 c.c. Hondas myself, so I know just how reliable these machines are.

All the basic Honda machines marketed from 1960 are covered in this book. They are the 50 c.c. models C.100, C.102, C.110, and C.114; the 125 c.c. models C.92 and CB.92; and the 250 c.c. models C.72 and CB.72. In addition, much of the data applicable to the C.100 range holds good for the "Monkey Bike" and the CE.105H Trials Bike; while the working instructions for the 250 c.c. models C.72 and CB.72 can also be applied to the 305 c.c. Models C.77 and CB.77. The recently-introduced C.200 (called for a short while the C.124) is not covered in detail, but owners of these models should still find the general working instructions in this book useful.

JOHN THORPE

CONTENTS

CHAPTER		PAGE
	Foreword	
	Preface	
I.	THE HONDA RANGE	1
II.	HANDLING HONDAS	3
III.	BASIC PRINCIPLES	9
IV.	FAULT TRACING	27
V.	TOOLS	41
VI.	GENERAL MAINTENANCE	44
VII.	MAINTAINING THE SINGLE-CYLINDER MODELS	50
VIII.	TOP OVERHAULS, SINGLES	64
IX.	WORKING ON THE TWINS	74
X.	ACCESSORIES FOR HONDAS	91
XI.	FUN FROM YOUR HONDA	93
	Appendix: FACTS AND FIGURES	97
	Index	103

CHAPTER I

THE HONDA RANGE

NEWCOMERS though they are, comparatively speaking, to the British scene Hondas have now become an extremely familiar sight on our roads. And rightly so, for these Oriental beauties have brought into the realm of utility riding the sort of engineering and finish which the cream of Europe's factories would be proud to claim. But there is nothing delicate about them—they are robustly reliable and capable of withstanding the hardest use.

Unquestionably the most popular model in the range (and almost without doubt the top-selling machine in this country today) is the C.100 —an overhead-valve 50 c.c. scooterette equipped with a three-speed gearbox and automatic clutch. It features a remarkably full specification— dual seating, full pillion equipment, front shielding in high-impact plastics, winking indicators, battery-boosted "electrics," and a tool kit which would shame many a car kit, let alone a scooter's!

This tough little fellow will put up road averages of around 32 miles an hour on give-and-take going, and on open roads is capable of about 45 m.p.h. Fuel consumptions may vary, according to conditions, from 110 to 150 m.p.g., and it will comfortably tackle hills as steep as 1 in 4. An electric-starter version is called the C.102; and the same engine unit is employed in the quaintly-named "Monkey Bike" which is a squat runabout designed to go into a car boot. There is also a cross-country development with a 55 c.c. engine, known as the CE.105H Trials model.

If these machines can be considered as small scooters, the associated C.110 and C.114 range of "50s" are true miniature motor-cycles. They have four-speed gearboxes with manual clutches, and also feature the unusually comprehensive electrical equipment which is a feature of the C.100. An 80 c.c. version, giving more power for pillion work, the C.124 was introduced for the 1964 season.

These are the only "singles" Honda produce. All other models in the range are twins. There is, for example, the 125 c.c. C.92 Benley, which must rate as one of the finest motor-cycles built anywhere in the world. It is powered by a parallel-twin overhead camshaft engine which gives it a top speed bettering 60 m.p.h. This peppy unit, allied to an exquisite four-speed gearbox and a frame and fork layout offering excellent handling, makes possible point-to-point averages of around 45 m.p.h. on open roads, compared with the 40 m.p.h. average speeds of the C.110. And there is a sports version—the CB.92—which is even quicker, though at the expense of a relatively austere specification.

For the tourist there is the Dream range of 250 and 305 c.c. models. The C.72 is very like an enlarged Benley, sharing with it a pressed-steel frame and swinging-link front fork. Its 305 c.c. counterpart is the C.77. Both are envisaged as luxury touring mounts, very completely equipped and softly sprung. Even so, the 250 c.c. version is capable of over 70 m.p.h.

Many people—myself certainly included—would rate the CB.72 Dream Super Sports as one of the great motor-cycles of all time. This wonderful machine embodies perfect handling and fantastic braking powers with the ability to reach around 85 m.p.h. in standard form. Its engine is a highly unusual o.h.c. parallel twin in which the cranks are set at an angle of 180° instead of the more conventional 360°. This gives excellent balance and an exhaust note which is curiously "lazy" for an engine which revs up to 9,000 r.p.m. in the intermediates. Averages of 60 m.p.h. are not impossible with this thoroughbred sports-tourer, and in production machine races it has on a number of occasions shown a clean pair of heels to machines of twice its capacity.

The "over-bored" CB.77, with its capacity of 305 c.c., offers the same top-end performance and championship-class handling, coupled with greater flexibility and faster acceleration.

Electric starting is common to all the twins, although amongst the singles it features only on the C.102. On the bigger models a 12-volt lighting system is used, giving an added boost to the Hondas' already very considerable safety factors.

Foot control is used for the gearboxes of all machines in the range. All are four-speeders apart from the "Monkey Bike," the Trials model, and the two scooterettes. Following a fairly common overseas practice the gear controls are mounted on the left and the footbrakes on the right. This is a peculiarity which is soon mastered.

With such a range of models to choose from, there is little doubt that more and more British riders will happily succumb to the sheer fascination of these superb Japanese machines. And there is every indication that the Trade shares the popular conviction that you cannot break a Honda, for secondhand prices show every sign of being higher than average, thus making a Honda an extremely attractive investment.

CHAPTER II

HANDLING HONDAS

THERE is an odd tradition that nobody needs to be taught how to handle a motor-cycle or scooterette. Newcomers to cars normally take a course of driving instruction. Would-be pilots need forty hours' tuition before they qualify. Even the highly non-mechanical sailing boat demands expert tuition before a novice can handle it. But for two-wheelers it is often thought sufficient for the purchaser to be shown the controls and then to be left to his or her own devices.

In some ways this is a reflection of the inherent safety and simplicity of the powered two-wheeler. And especially with machines as soundly designed and constructed as the Hondas the safety factor is very high indeed. Self-tuition is certainly possible, but such is the crowded state of our roads today that it is no longer the best way of learning a new art. And an art it is, the handling of a responsive motor-cycle.

In some parts of the country it is possible to enrol for a course in the R.A.C./A.-C.U. Learner Training Scheme. This consists of a series of a dozen riding lessons and a dozen lectures in a course which lasts twelve weeks. The instruction is given by members of A.-C.U. clubs—real enthusiasts, who love motor-cycling and are happy to pass on their "know-how" to the newcomer so that he, too, will become not only a proficient rider but an enthusiast also. For make no mistake about it, once you have become a real motor-cyclist no other form of transport will ever really supplant it in your affections. Even if you never intend to do more than ride to and from work you will find that every trip is an enjoyable outing.

All the initial instruction takes place on private ground. When the instructor feels that the pupil is able to handle his machine well enough the lessons continue on public roads, and at the end of the course it is possible to take a test for a proficiency certificate. Unfortunately this does not, as yet, absolve one from the necessity of taking the M.o.T. Driving Test, but possession of the certificate certainly gives one confidence in one's ability to pass the test first time.

As the training scheme is voluntary it does not operate in all parts of the country, but there is a fairly constant expansion and the Manager of the R.A.C. Motor-cycle Department at 85 Pall Mall, London, S.W.1, is always prepared to put inquirers into touch with their nearest centre. The cost—only thirty-six shillings at the outside—plus, of course, what you spend on petrol getting there. It is a wise investment.

Where no training scheme centre is handy self-tuition must of necessity fill the gap. The danger here is that bad habits may unwittingly be formed, and they become increasingly difficult to break. The riding style which the learner evolves at this stage is likely to remain with him, substantially unaltered, throughout his riding life. It determines not only whether he becomes a safe and skilled rider, but also whether he is one who gives his machine an easy life or whether he becomes an habitual "wrecker." Much wear and tear on the bike—and a considerable amount of time- and money-consuming mechanical tinkering—can be saved by riding habits alone, providing they are good ones!

Start your studies in an armchair, learning all about your machine and its controls. Having memorized the location of each of them (including the various switches controlling the main and dipped beams, the winkers, the horn, and so forth) close your eyes and pretend you are on the machine. Then give yourself a series of quick tests, for example: "Apply the front brake," "Signal a right turn," "Dip the lights," and so on. Make the appropriate hand movement at the same time, so that you eventually operate the controls almost as quickly as you can think.

When you have memorized all the controls and have finished your course of armchair instruction go outside to the machine, sit on it, and go through the entire exercise again. But in each case *do it with your eyes shut*. The reason is simple. On the road you will not have time to look down to see where your controls are. The place for your eyes is on the road ahead. Your hands and feet must be able to find the appropriate controls unaided.

The next step is to learn how to start the engine and how to control it once it is going. Switch on the petrol and, for the first start of the day, depress the float chamber tickler for about five seconds. If the air temperature is low you may also need to close or partly close the choke control too. Keep the Honda on its stand and get astride the machine. Switch on the ignition, check that the neutral warning light is on to show you that the gears are not engaged, and open the twistgrip throttle about an eighth of an inch. On a C.100, C.110 or C.114 you will have to kickstart. Do this by placing the ball of the foot on the starter and thrusting downwards in an arc so that the starter is taken progressively down to the end of its stroke. Don't just jab—the aim is to give a steady thrust. On all other models you will need only to press the starter button and the engine should start almost at once. Let it warm for a minute or so and then open the choke fully.

Now sit on your machine and spend a few minutes gently opening and closing the throttle so that you become accustomed to the way the machine responds. Don't jerk it open—just revolve the grip smoothly a fraction of an inch at a time, noting how the engine speeds up as you do so. Don't allow it to race. As there is no load on it, the motor will speed up very quickly indeed, and a sharp burst of throttle could cause it to over-rev and damage the valve gear. All you need to do is to accustom yourself to the feel of the control and learn how to operate it smoothly to avoid jerky progress when you start to ride.

You are now ready to make your first excursion. If you have access to a private drive—or, in the country, if a farmer will let you into a fallow field—then by all means make use of it. If not, choose a quiet road where other traffic will neither endanger you nor be endangered by you. And, if it is at all possible, keep well away from houses so that residents are not annoyed by your short trips up and down the street. It is well worth while pushing the machine a mile or so to a suitable site if you are not sure enough of yourself to ride it there, rather than take risks at this stage.

One of your main difficulties will be mastering the delicate operation of the clutch and its co-ordination with the throttle—unless, of course, you have a C.100 or C.102, both of which have automatic clutches. But with all other models practise "take-offs" first of all. This can be done by standing astride the machine, both feet firmly on the ground, and starting the engine. Then pull out the clutch lever, engage first gear, and slowly release the lever again by unfolding the fingers of your left hand from the knuckles, not from the finger joints, for the first inch or so of lever travel. This is done fairly quickly, but as you feel the drive begin to take up and the Honda move forward check the action immediately. This condition, with the clutch still not fully engaged and therefore still slipping, is necessary during the initial moving-off period—otherwise the engine would simply stall as the full load was suddenly applied.

Withdraw the clutch again, select neutral, release the clutch, and wait for a few seconds before repeating the experiment. This ensures that you will not overwork the clutch during this essential practising period. Then go through the procedure again until you are certain that you can recognize the instant when the drive begins to take up, and can check your clutch hand movement accurately at that point. Once this initial movement has been mastered you should be able to make reasonably smooth get-aways each time.

With the C.100 and C.102 the problem is easier—you have merely to be able to recognize when the drive is taking itself up and get your feet onto the footrests as the machine moves away. Try a few standing starts by having the engine ticking over, engaging first or second gear, and then gently opening the throttle. As the engine speeds up the clutch will begin to engage and the scooterette will move forward. Get your feet up at once if you plan to ride on, or, if you are just practising, close the throttle and apply the front brake. There are no snags, but it is important to remember that the automatic clutch is coupled in three different ways and that one of these is to the gear-change pedal. Holding the pedal down with the foot will thus keep the clutch disengaged and releasing it suddenly can cause a most disconcerting "bunny-jump." *Always* release the pedal fully immediately you have selected a gear.

These two machines also differ from the rest of the range in having only three-speed gearboxes and in the use of a positive "neutral" located between first and second gears. The theory is logical enough. Top and second gears give an adequate spread for all normal riding, including moving off. Use the machine as a two-speeder, and you have neutral readily available and easy to find. The neutral indicator light helps to ensure this too. In the unusual event of an extra-heavy load being carried, or a really steep hill needing to be climbed, you still have an "emergency low" gear beyond neutral. In practice the idea works well, though for optimum acceleration I have found that it is best to use the Honda as a normal three-speeder and make the necessary double change to go straight from first gear to second. A learner might be better advised to stick to the "two speeds plus" philosophy.

When you are certain that you can get your machine on the move without jerks and without screaming the engine at unnecessarily high revs you are ready for the next stage—your first excursion under power. Choose a quiet stretch of road, if possible, and get under way in first gear. Don't bother to change up—just concentrate on controlling your speed by use of the throttle. With the automatic clutch models, though, don't travel *too* slowly or you will find that the clutch will disengage.

Practise speed control with the twist grip until you can accelerate and decelerate smoothly. When you come to the end of your stretch of road either try your hand at a controlled turn under power or, if you are not yet sufficiently confident, get into neutral and wheel the machine round.

The next step will be to learn how to make your turn at the end of each run (don't forget to make your signals). Then you will be able to start using the gears as well. First of all try changing from first into second and back throughout the run. Then bring the other gears into use as well. Learn one thing at a time until you can start the engine, get away, engage top gear, decelerate, and turn smoothly.

With the motor-cycles, you will have to acquire the necessary co-ordination between hands and feet which alone will enable you to operate the gears and control the speed to a nicety. To change from a low gear to a high gear, for example, you will have to make several movements simultaneously—or virtually so. First, the throttle is snapped shut and the clutch is drawn out, the two hands—right and left—working as one. As the clutch is disengaged the left foot operates the gear control, and as soon as the gear has been selected the clutch is released and the throttle re-opened. The object is to make the change as quickly as you can.

To change down, the easiest method is to withdraw the clutch and, almost at once, operate the gear pedal. At the same time the throttle is given a quick blip to raise the engine speed and so ease engagement. Purists prefer to make a clean change by leaving the throttle opening constant and letting the engine speed rise as the change is made, judging the whole procedure to a nicety so that there is no noticeable change in engine note throughout. That is a skill worth acquiring as you gain in experience, but during this early stage it is perhaps better to use blipped changes.

Both when moving off and when coming to rest the place for your feet is on the footrests. It is a bad mistake to leave the feet to "trail" for an instant longer than necessary, since you are not properly balanced on your machine till your feet are up.

On take-off the feet should be raised as soon as the clutch begins to "bite," and, when halting, one foot (and one foot only) should be grounded just a fraction of a second before the machine actually comes to rest. Trailing feet are the mark of a motor-cycling illiterate.

Many learners, especially where only pedal cycles have been used before, make the mistake of using only the rear brake and ignoring the front brake. This is incorrect, for the front brake is the more effective of the two and it is far less likely to provide a skid under bad conditions. Skilled riders use the front brake almost exclusively for checking speed when making a turn, and for stopping they give it a slight lead over the rear brake.

The reason is simple. When the rear brake is applied the effect on the machine is to transfer the weight forward. The loading on the rear wheel therefore decreases, and so does its adhesion. By contrast, this weight transfer adds to the load on the front wheel and therefore improves its adhesion. Therefore try to use both brakes in unison. If you *have* acquired a rear-brake-only complex, break yourself of it at this formative stage by using only the front brake for making all practice stops (though both should be employed for emergencies, of course). This will enable you to get the feel of the front brake—though it should be remembered that both brakes will tend to gain in power once they have lost their initial newness and start bedding-in properly.

To brake hard, the initial movement is to flick the throttle shut and follow-through this right hand movement by grasping the front brake lever and applying gentle hand pressure. At the same time the right foot begins to press on the rear brake pedal. Both pressures are steadily increased as the machine slows, and as it comes to a standstill the clutch, too, is withdrawn. The result is a quick straight-line stop.

Great care must be taken when the roads are slippery. Under these conditions I prefer to slow against the compression of the engine and use the brakes only sparingly to "kill" the last few miles an hour. Slowing in this way involves nothing more complicated than closing the throttle and, possibly, dropping down through the gears. To keep the speed in check if I am descending a steep hill with a treacherous surface I also give just the barest tickle on the front brake. This must be done gently—the object is merely to prevent the machine accelerating, not to stop it.

A two-wheeler is steered by being leaned to one side or the other so that the balanced forces holding it in equilibrium are upset by the arrival of a third force. Unopposed, this third force would simply cause the machine to topple over, but the very act of leaning it forces it into a turn and a fourth factor—centrifugal force—then comes into play. The result is that the machine stays banked at an angle and goes smoothly round the corner. If a turn was initiated with the machine upright, there would be nothing but the friction between the tyres and the road to prevent centrifugal force dragging it bodily across the road away from the centre on the turn.

For each combination of radius of turn and speed there is thus an ideal angle of bank, but luckily it is not necessary to go to the trouble of having rate-of-turn meters and inclinometers to ensure that all is well—the rider can *feel* whether or not the machine is turning smoothly and can increase or decrease the angle of bank to suit the case.

Most of the work of cornering has, in fact, to be done before the corner is reached. The object—simply stated, if not so simply achieved—is to arrive at the corner at the right speed, in the right gear, on the right point on the road.

As the Honda comes towards a corner its rider has to weigh up the pattern of the road and decide how to tackle the turn. All the braking and slowing has to be done with the machine upright and this, therefore, is completed on the approach. The first stage is to lose just the right amount of speed and to get into the right gear. What gear this is depends on the circumstances and on the machine.

The approach to the corner is made in the selected gear, with the throttle either fully or partly closed. If necessary, the brakes can also be applied. It is heeled over to take the bend, and as the rider reaches the point when he can see all that lies ahead the throttle is opened gently and the machine taken through under power. As the model is straightened up the power is increased and the exit is made under acceleration and at a higher speed than was used on the approach.

Make your golden rule for cornering the one which every racing man learns by heart: "In slow; out fast." Otherwise, you may have an unpleasant acquaintance with the second half of that saying: "In fast; out feet first." And on the road there is even less need than in racing to take any risks.

CHAPTER III

BASIC PRINCIPLES

METICULOUS attention to design, as well as superb production engineering, has made the Honda motor-cycles the top-class models that they are. But to obtain the best from his machine the rider, too, has got to put something into the common pool. And to make his contribution he must know what makes it tick.

Only four-stroke engines are produced by Honda. This term "four-stroke" refers to the number of working strokes in one complete cycle of operation of the engine. In the four-stroke power unit, a working cycle

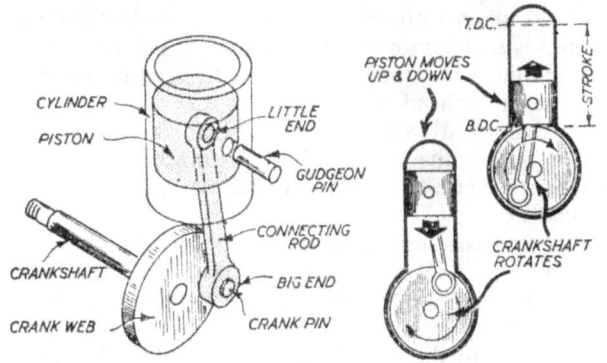

FIG. 1. THE BASIC PARTS OF A SINGLE-CYLINDER INTERNAL COMBUSTION ENGINE

(From *The Book of the B.S.A. Sunbeam and Triumph Tigress*.)

consists of four distinct strokes—in other words the piston travels from its uppermost position to its lowest, or vice versa, four times. Each cycle, therefore, comprises two downward and two upward strokes.

Before considering these in detail, however, let's get our bearings and assign names to the major engine components. The basis of the Honda engines—as of all reciprocating internal-combustion engines—is the crankshaft. This is basically a set of flywheels (two in the case of the singles; four in the twins) which are supported by main shafts projecting from the centre of each outer flywheel. These shafts are themselves carried on main bearings, mounted in an alloy container which is called the crank-case.

Joining the flywheels is a crank pin. This is not mounted concentrically, like the main shafts, but is set towards the outer edge of the wheels. So, if the wheels are revolved the main shafts merely go round and round. The movement of the crank pin, on the other hand, follows the circumference of a circle whose radius is the distance between the centre of the main shafts and the centre of the crank pin.

This "bottom half" assembly forms the rotating parts of the engine. But the power is produced, basically, by the reciprocating parts—those which move up and down. The two sections have a common member in the connecting rod, whose job is to transmit the reciprocating movement of the piston to the crank assembly for conversion to useful rotary movement.

The connecting rod is pivoted on the crank pin, friction here being reduced by a bearing which is known as the "big end." The reason is not far to seek—it is, in fact, the bigger end of the connecting rod. At the other end of the rod is another bearing—the "small end," through which passes the gudgeon pin. This is the pivot on which the piston is held.

Made of light alloy, with split steel piston rings to ensure a close fit, the piston spends its life moving up and down inside the cylinder, which is bolted to the mouth of the crankcase. Closing the other end of the cylinder is the cylinder head, which contains a hemispherical combustion chamber. In this are a pair of poppet valves which are automatically opened and closed so that combustible mixture can be drawn into the engine and burned gases expelled. It also has a sparking plug which ignites the mixture.

Having got our basic engine, let's see how it works. Imagine that the piston is at the top of its stroke—at top dead centre (which is usually abbreviated to T.D.C.) and that we are just about to start up. Whether it is done with the self-starter or with the kick starter makes no difference. Both are connected to the mainshaft, and operation of either turns the shaft in the normal working direction.

As the shaft begins to turn, the crank pin (being offset) moves forward and downwards for the first quarter revolution and then backwards and downwards for the second quarter. During the whole of this first half revolution it draws the piston down the cylinder.

All the time, the inlet valve has been open. As the movement of the piston has created a relatively low pressure inside the cylinder, the higher pressure of the outside atmosphere has forced a mixture of fuel and air through the inlet port and into the cylinder, so by the time the piston reaches the end of its travel—bottom dead centre, or B.D.C.—the cylinder is filled with inflammable gas. This stroke is therefore called the induction stroke.

It is not enough, though, for the mixture to be inflammable. To produce combustion which is fast enough for the purpose of driving an engine it must first be compressed. That is the purpose of the compression stroke,

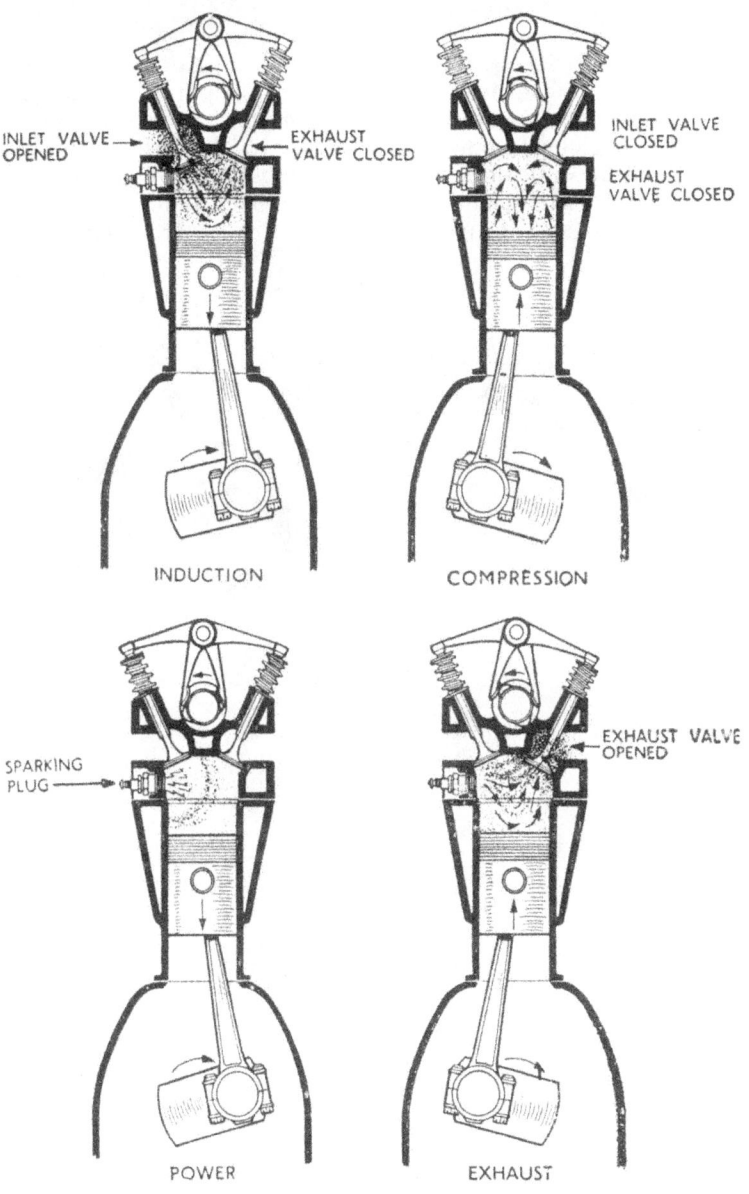

FIG. 2. THE PRINCIPLE OF THE FOUR-STROKE CYCLE BEHIND ALL HONDA ENGINES
Top: Induction and Compression strokes; *bottom:* Power and Exhaust strokes.
(From *The Internal Combustion Engine* by Staton Abbey.)

which follows. First, the inlet valve is closed so that the gas is trapped in the cylinder. Then—driven by the energy stored in the flywheels—the piston begins to rise up the cylinder. Crank pin movement during this second half revolution is upwards and backwards during the first quarter; upwards and forwards during the second, until at T.D.C. the crank pin has returned to its original position. By the time this has happened and the piston is at T.D.C., the mixture will have been compressed into a space

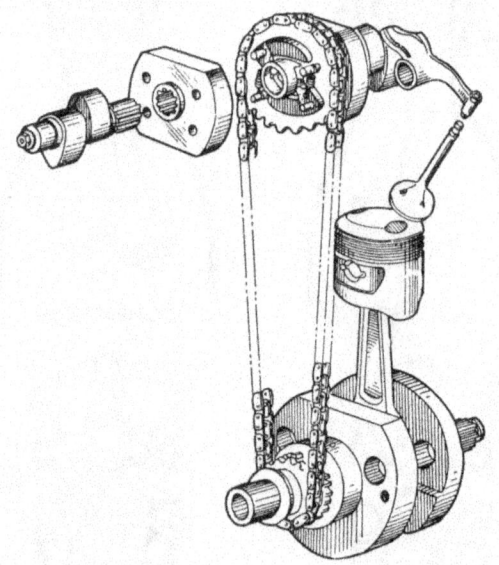

FIG. 3. HOW AN OVERHEAD CAMSHAFT WORKS

All the twin-cylinder Hondas use this type of valve gear. The camshaft is mounted in the cylinder head and is driven by a chain from the crankshaft.

perhaps only one-eighth or one-tenth as big as that which it originally occupied. Now, it will burn rapidly when ignited.

This is done at or about T.D.C. by an electrical spark which jumps over the points of the sparking plug. The resultant rapid burning causes the gases inside the cylinder to expand, exerting heavy pressures on all the surrounding surfaces. Of these, only one can move—the top of the piston. Consequently, the gases drive the piston rapidly down the cylinder and the connecting rod, now driving the flywheel instead of being driven by it, thrusts on the crank pin and so turns the main shafts under power. This is the power stroke.

As the piston approaches the end of this stroke the exhaust valve is opened and on the ensuing upward stroke the burned gases are driven out of the cylinder. This is consequently called the exhaust stroke.

BASIC PRINCIPLES   13

This, then, is the basic cycle—induction, compression, power, exhaust. Towards the end of the exhaust stroke the inlet valve begins to open again, and a new cycle of operations begins. In the Honda engines, at top speed, the cycle can be repeated up to 5,000 times every minute in each cylinder.

In practice, the strokes are not quite as well-defined as this. Though the gas streams are light they—like every other form of matter—still possess inertia. They take a few milli-seconds to get on the move, or to change direction once they are moving. Consequently, a certain amount of overlap is allowed for at the end of the exhaust stroke and the beginning of the induction stroke, and at the end of the power stroke.

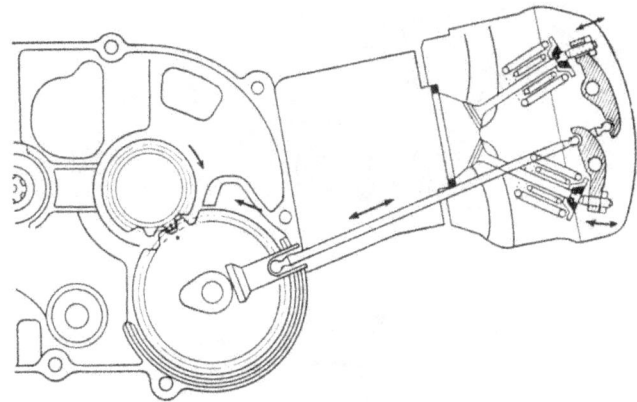

FIG. 4. THE OVERHEAD VALVE LAYOUT ON SINGLES
Honda single-cylinder power units, while still having overhead valves, use push-rod operation to open them. How it works is shown in this diagram.

As the piston approaches B.D.C. on the power stroke, for example, the exhaust valve is opened. True, this sacrifices a modicum of power, although there is very little energy left in the gases by this time. This sacrifice is more than recouped by the fact that the gases start to leave the cylinder under their own pressure. This reduces the amount of work that the piston has to do to expel them as the exhaust stroke gets under way.

While the piston is still travelling upwards on the last part of the exhaust stroke the inlet valve is opened. This does not result in the stale gas being pumped into the inlet port—it is already moving too quickly into the relatively low-pressure area of the exhaust pipe for that—but it *does* give the inlet gas stream a chance to get on the move before the induction stroke proper begins.

All this, of course, argues very precise control over the valves. In the 50 c.c. Honda engines the valves are operated through rockers and push-rods—an overhead valve arrangement. The more powerful twins use rockers on which the camshaft bears direct—an overhead camshaft arrangement. In each case, the contours of the cams determine the behaviour of the valves. A cam can be regarded as a wheel which has been deliberately distorted so that instead of rolling smoothly it has an up and down action. Anybody who has ridden a bicycle with a wheel out of true knows what happens. As the machine moves along the front or rear end continually rises or falls as the unevenly radiused wheel revolves.

The action of a cam is similar, save that the camshaft is held rigidly in position and cannot move up or down. The movement is therefore

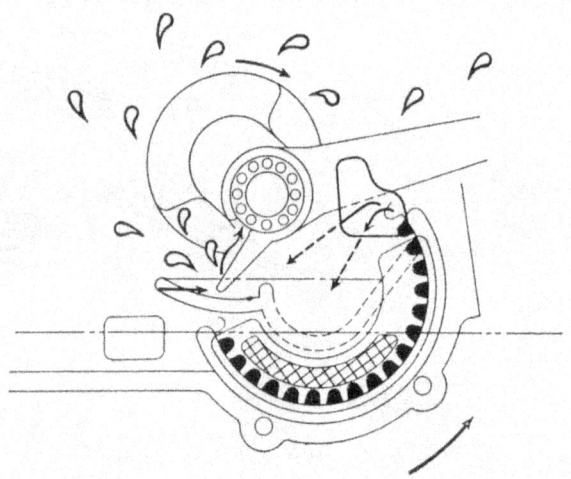

FIG. 5. WET SUMP LUBRICATION ON THE SINGLES

The rotating cam gear feeds oil from the reservoir to the sump in the crankcase. It is scooped up and splashed to the cylinder, piston, and crank bearings.

transmitted to the surface which is in contact with the cam periphery—to a tappet block in the case of the o.h.v. motor, and direct to one end of a rocker in the o.h.c. engine. As the cam rotates these parts reciprocate. The tappet block transmits its movement to a pushrod which itself bears on one end of a rocker. In each case the rocker see-saws about a central pivot, so that the other end either depresses or releases the stem of its valve. These valves are, of course, spring-loaded, so that they are normally held tightly shut.

A further vital part of the four-stroke engine is the oil pump. The lower part of the crankcase—the sump—contains a supply of lubricating oil, whose purpose is to reduce friction between the various components of the engine and to help absorb internal heat. Some of the oil is distributed, in the form of a mist, simply by the splash effect created by the revolving

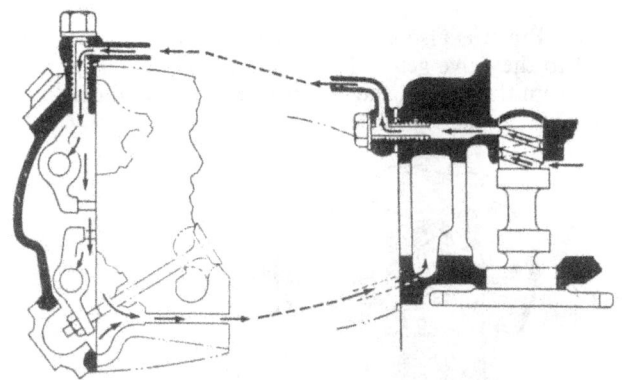

Fig. 6. Rocker Box Lubrication System

The camshaft is used as a pump to force oil through the external pipe to the rocker box. Afterwards, it is returned to the sump through tunnels.

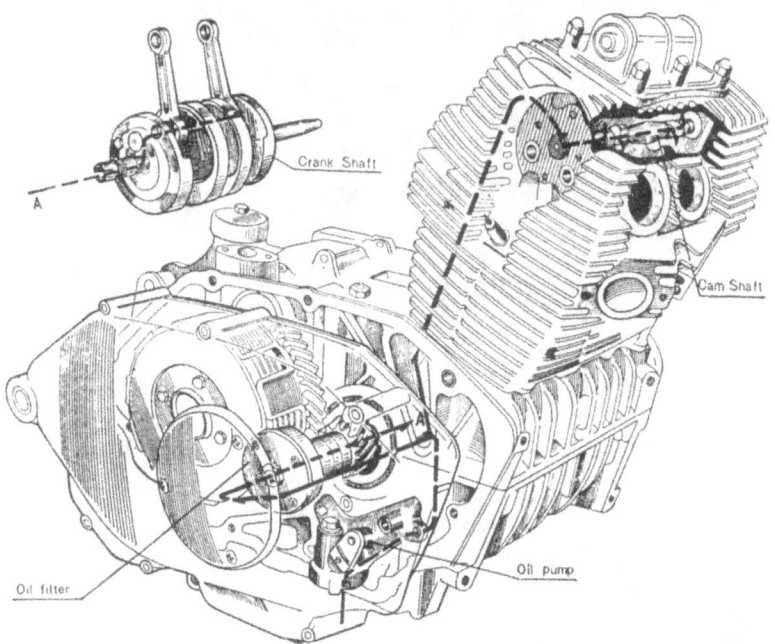

Fig. 7. Lubrication System on 125 c.c. Twins

internal parts. But it is also essential that it is taken to the vital big-end bearings and to the valve gear. This is the job of the oil pump. Driven by a linkage from the engine, the pump sucks in oil and drives it through internal passages to the more heavily-stressed areas. Its job done it is

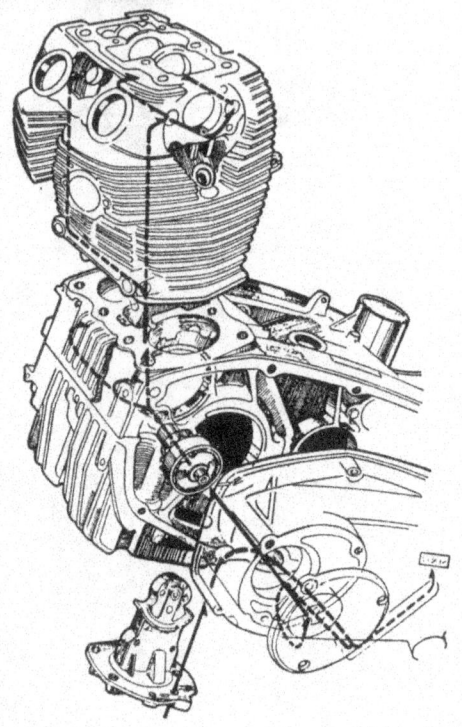

FIG. 8. LUBRICATION SYSTEM ON 250 C.C. TWINS

allowed to fall back into the sump, where it has a chance to cool again before being pumped through the system once more.

THE IGNITION SYSTEM

Often, even experienced riders have only the slightest knowledge of the working of the electrical system upon which the whole operation of the engine depends. As a result the electrics tend to be neglected until failure results, when the assumption is made that "electrickery" is an unreliable thing anyway!

However, there is no need to be a qualified electrical engineer to understand *how* the system works, even if the actual reasons behind it have to be taken for granted.

BASIC PRINCIPLES

All electrical practice is founded upon circuits and upon the fact that an electric current will invariably take the shortest path to earth. In this connexion it should be emphasized that "earth" does not necessarily mean the ground. So far as a Honda's electrical system is concerned "earth" is the mass of the machine itself.

A circuit is just what its name implies. In this, electricity is rather like a model railway train. If all the points are correctly set the train will go round and round. If they are not so set it will simply end up standing still on a siding. Or it may be routed on to a damaged line and so derail itself.

As with the train, so with electricity. Providing there is a circuit the current will flow; if the circuit is broken it will not. And a bad points setting—a short circuit—may direct it straight to earth.

Electricity is measured in volts and amperes. The volt is a measure of its electrical force; the ampere is basically a measure of the number of electrons per second passing a given point.

So while voltage indicates the electrical pressure, amperage shows what quantity of current is flowing. The resistance to the current flow inherent in the wires and so forth which make up the physical side of the system is measured in ohms, one ohm being a resistance which calls for one volt to be applied so that one ampere may flow.

Electricity is further regarded as comprising two basic types of current —positive and negative—but for all practical purposes it is necessary only to know that these exist. Finally, one must accept a single basic fact— that when a coil is placed within a magnetic field electricity is produced in its windings.

On most Hondas, the main electricity supply comes from an a.c. generator which is driven directly by the engine crankshaft. A battery —charged by the generator through the medium of a selenium rectifier— is provided to give additional current when the demand rises above the output of the generator.

The ignition system comprises the generator and battery, a form of mechanical switch known as the contact breaker (together with its associated advance/retard mechanism), a condenser, a coil, two sparking plugs, and the associated leads and switchgear.

Primary current is supplied from the electrical system to the low-tension side of the ignition system. This comprises the contact breaker, the condenser, and the low-tension windings of the coil. These windings surround a high-tension winding, but are not in contact with it—they are insulated from it.

Here is where the actual happenings inside the system have to be taken on trust. While current is flowing through the low-tension windings, there is none whatsoever in the high-tension system. But as soon as the low-tension current is broken—which is the job of the contact breaker—the result is to generate a high-tension current in the secondary windings

In the case of the Honda this current is in the region of between 15,000 and 20,000 volts. Seeking the shortest path to earth, this current races down the heavily-insulated ignition lead, which is connected to the central electrode of the sparking plug.

Now the plug's central electrode would, normally speaking, be an electrical dead end, since it is not connected to earth or a circuit and is separated from the plug's side electrode by a gap of some 0·025 of an inch.

A low-tension current would, in fact, stop short at the gap. But the high-tension current has such force behind it that it cannot do so. Instead, it leaps across it in the form of a hot blue spark, and it is this spark which ignites the mixture.

As this happens some 5,000 times each minute in each cylinder it is obvious that pretty accurate timing is required. This is provided by the contact breaker, whose opening and closing is controlled by a cam on the engine's main shaft or on the camshaft.

Of the two contact breaker points one is carried on a plate, the other on a centre-pivoting arm. The far end of this arm has a heel which bears on the cam. Consequently, as the cam revolves the arm see-saws and the points open and close. To prevent the low-tension current from backfiring and bridging the points while the gap is small an electrical shock-absorber—the condenser—is added to the low-tension circuit. This is virtually a one-way valve, for it allows electricity to pass through to the primary windings of the coil but not to surge back from them.

Obviously, fast though electricity may travel—and it speeds through the wires at 186,000 miles per second—there is still a time-lag in all this. And the engine does not run at a constant speed. The C.92, for example, can run happily in top gear at any engine speed between 1,700 r.p.m. and some 9,500 r.p.m. If the spark were to occur at a fixed time it would entail the use of a compromise setting, rather than one which was ideal for each engine speed. Thus a spark which was occurring in good time to get the best possible combustion at, say, 5,000 r.p.m. could be early at 2,000 r.p.m. and late at 9,000 r.p.m. To this, the automatic advance/retard mechanism applies at least a partial solution. This is, basically, a series of spring-loaded weights attached to the cam mechanism. As the engine speed increases the weights, under the pull of centrifugal force, fly outwards. As the revs decrease, the spring pulls them back. In each case, the movement so obtained is used to twist the cam backwards or forwards relative to the shaft. The spark is therefore made to occur earlier or later, depending upon the rotational speed of the engine. On the 125 c.c. C.92 twin, for example, the initial setting has the spark timed to occur 5° before T.D.C. At maximum speed, this timing has altered to 40° before T.D.C.

The C.100 scooterette has the simpler flywheel magneto type of ignition in which the coils are contained within the flywheel itself, on a back plate which also bears the contact breaker and condenser. Here, the electricity is generated by the effect of the rotation of magnets fixed into the periphery of the flywheel and no provision is made for altering the timing which, in this case, is set to 55° B.T.D.C. The C.102 version, on the other hand, has a.c. type electrical equipment and automatic variation of the spark between 5° and 55° B.T.D.C.

THE CARBURETTOR

So far one vital part of the power unit has not been considered. We noted in passing only that when air is induced into the cylinder it is mixed with petrol to form a combustible mixture. And that was a drastic understatement of the work done by a simple but precisely-engineered instrument known as the carburettor.

In principle this may seem to be little more than a glorified scent spray with a fancy name. But it has to carry out one of the most exacting of all tasks—metering a minute quantity of petrol and mixing it thoroughly with air in just the right proportions for efficient burning.

At first this may not seem over-exacting, since the ideal ratio is roughly 1 part of petrol to 14 parts of air by weight. The carburettor, however, does not operate by weight but by volume. On this basis, each 50 c.c. of combustible mixture needs to contain only 0·005 c.c. of petrol. The remaining 49·995 c.c. is all air, so the proportion actually metered by the carburettor is nearly 1 part of petrol to 10,000 parts of air. Obviously, despite its simple design, a carburettor is a precision instrument and needs to be treated as such.

The basic components of a carburettor are a petrol reservoir, called a float chamber; a venturi, or choke, through which air is drawn; jets, which meter the petrol; and a throttle, which controls the amount of mixture passing through the instrument.

First consider the basic method of operation. Petrol is fed to the float chamber, which is much like a pocket edition of the domestic cistern. It contains a float (a double float in the case of the bigger Hondas) which rises as petrol is admitted through a valve. In doing so the float presses the valve's tapered needle upwards. As this needle is carefully contoured to fit in the valve seat it gradually shuts off the fuel supply, and when the preset level has been reached no more fuel can enter the chamber until the engine uses a proportion of the supply already there and the level falls, the float sinks with it, the needle valve opens, and more fuel flows in until the correct level is again attained.

Connecting the float chamber with the body of the carburettor is a drilled passageway through which the fuel can flow into a jet well. Obviously, the level in the well is controlled by the level in the float chamber. Immersed in the fuel in the well is a jet. This is screwed into the end of a needle jet tube, the other end of which opens into the venturi.

This jet looks suspiciously like a small bolt with a hole drilled through its centre. In fact that is just what it is—but the hole is so proportioned that it will pass just the right amount of fuel and no more.

When the induction stroke begins in the cylinder air is drawn through the carburettor venturi. This is so shaped that as this air passes through there is a fall in pressure in the section into which the jet tube projects. As a result, petrol from the jet well rises up the needle jet, passes into the air stream as a fine spray, and mixes with the air in a section of the venturi called the mixing chamber. From there, it passes down the inlet tract and into the cylinder.

Obviously, a carburettor which contained only these parts would work, but would pass the same amount of fuel and air under all conditions. Consequently the engine would run at a fixed speed. Since the engine speed must be variable so, too, must the amount of fuel and air which enters through the carburettor. This is done by adding to the basic layout just described a throttle slide and a needle. The needle is clipped to the throttle slide, and projects below it to enter the needle jet. The throttle slide is barrel shaped, and has a moon-shaped cutaway in its leading edge to govern the amount of air which can be admitted at intermediate throttle openings. The combined effect of this cutaway and of the tapered needle is to restrict air and fuel flow proportionately. The slide/needle assembly is so arranged that it is raised when a throttle control is opened and lowered as the control is shut. The more the throttle is opened the higher the slide is lifted and the more air it permits to pass. Since the needle is attached to the slide this, too, is lifted in the jet tube. The tube is tapered internally, and raising the needle therefore increases the effective volume of the tube, enabling a greater amount of fuel to pass into the venturi.

For idling only a small quantity of air is admitted through the cutaway and under the rear edge of the slide, which is held partly open by an adjustable throttle stop. The amount involved is too small for effective metering by the needle jet, and this is therefore closed completely. Instead, a minute quantity of fuel is by-passed through internal drillings to emerge behind the venturi and mix with the air there, so giving a pilot supply for idling.

Starting from cold requires a richer mixture than usual—that is one with a greater proportion of petrol to air. This is obtained, in the case of the twins, by incorporating an auxiliary air slide. Lowering the slide reduces the intake of air and, the supply of petrol being unchanged, gives a richer mixture. On 50 c.c. engines a pivoted butterfly choke is used instead to obtain the same effect.

As proper operation of the carburettor depends upon the action of fine metering devices all fuel is filtered before it enters the instrument. It is essential that this standard of cleanliness is maintained at all times, for even a microscopic speck of grit can block a jet and lead to weak mixtures and consequent overheating.

The air filter, on the other hand, is intended primarily to protect the engine's internals by filtering out sharp specks of dirt which are present in air. An air filter acts as an obstacle to the air flow, and thereby cuts

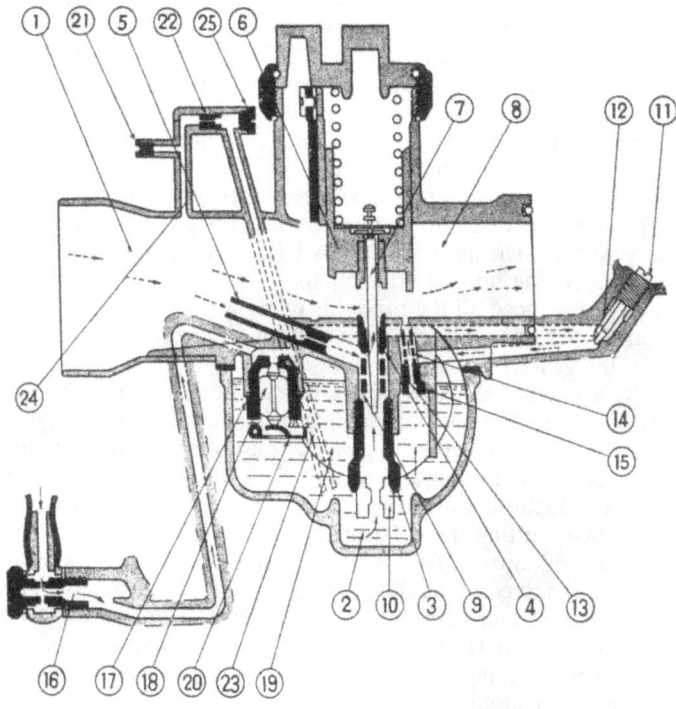

Fig. 9. Layout of a Keihin Carburettor

1. Venturi.
2. Float chamber.
3. Needle jet holder.
4. Needle jet.
5. Air bleed.
6. Throttle slide.
7. Needle.
8. Mixing chamber.
9. Air bleed outlets.
10. Main jet.
11. Pilot air screw.
12. Pilot air orifice.
13. Slow-running jet.
14. Bleed holes.
15. Slow-running jet orifice.
16. Banjo union.
17. Needle valve seat.
18. Valve needle.
19. Float.
20. Float arm.
21. Power air jet.
22. Power jet.
23. Power jet fuel pipe.
24. Power nozzle.
25. Plug screw.

the amount which enters the carburettor. If for any reason, then, the filter is removed more air will enter. If the fuel supply is unchanged the result, again, will be a weak mixture. Damage to the engine interior apart, this is one good reason why the motor should never be run without its cleaner, unless the jets, etc., are suitably modified to suit the new conditions.

TRANSMISSION

Motor-cycle power units are high-speed engines, in which the power output is, within limits, proportional to the speed of rotation of the crankshaft. At low engine speeds less power is developed than at high speeds. Where outside factors, such as a hill or a stiff head wind, increase the load on the machine its crankshaft speed—and therefore its power—falls off. This, in turn, reduces the speed still further, leading to a consistent drop in power until, at length, the engine can no longer pull against the load imposed and it stalls.

Basically, maximum power is developed over a comparatively narrow engine speed range and the engine should, ideally, run at this speed wherever possible. The designer usually tries to arrange for this "torque" peak to occur at the normal cruising speed, but as no road vehicle can run at a constant speed all the time it is necessary to have some means of compensating for changing loads at differing speeds. And that is the purpose of the gearbox.

Basically, a gearbox consists of a series of meshing gears—three pairs in the scooterettes, four on the remaining machines in the range. Pairs of gears can be locked together to give a choice of three (or four) different reductions between the input and output sides of the box.

Initially, a reduction is made in the primary drive between the engine and the gearbox, cutting the rotational speed but increasing the effective torque, or turning effort. This is because the number of power strokes per revolution is increased as the gearing is lowered. Inside the gearbox itself selector forks, controlled by the gear change through a positive-stop mechanism (except on Hondas intended for the Japanese home market which use a rotary change), move gears sideways, so that dogs on their sides can engage or disengage.

The result is to give the rider a choice of ratios, one of which will almost certainly bring the engine speed into line with the load. On the 250 c.c. C.72, for example, top gear is a direct drive, whereas bottom gear has a reduction of 3·39:1. When the effect of primary and secondary drive reductions—for the final chain drive, too, is geared down—is taken into account the rider can choose between overall gears from 6·59:1 in top to 22·35:1 in bottom gear.

In effect, this means that in top gear the crankshaft will revolve six and a half times in one revolution of the rear wheel. Consequently, seven power strokes will be applied in that distance. In bottom gear, the crankshaft will revolve nearly twenty-two and a half times, and in the same distance—one revolution of the rear wheel—the power of twenty-three firing strokes can be brought to bear. Obviously, greater power can be applied in bottom gear—but at the expense of speed as there is a definite limit to the number of power strokes the engine can produce in a given time.

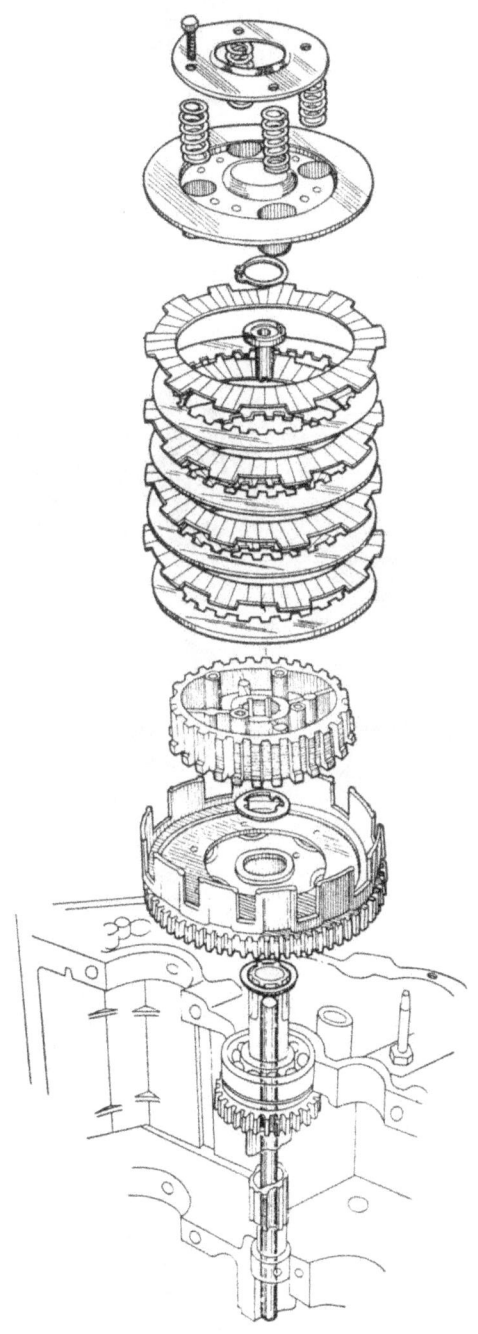

FIG. 10. A TYPICAL MULTI-PLATE CLUTCH
This is the type of clutch used on the 125 c.c. C.92 motor-cycle.

A vital part of the transmission is the clutch, which enables the drive to be freed. A clutch consists of a series of plates. These are alternately plain and friction-lined. And alternate plates vary in the manner of their fixing inside the clutch body. Some of the plates have plain circular centre cutaways, but are splined on their outer periphery. The others have plain circumferences, but have splines projecting into the centre cutouts. The former type mate with slots cut in the drum-like clutch body; the latter mate up with splines on the clutch centre.

The clutch body is driven by the engine's primary drive gear, but

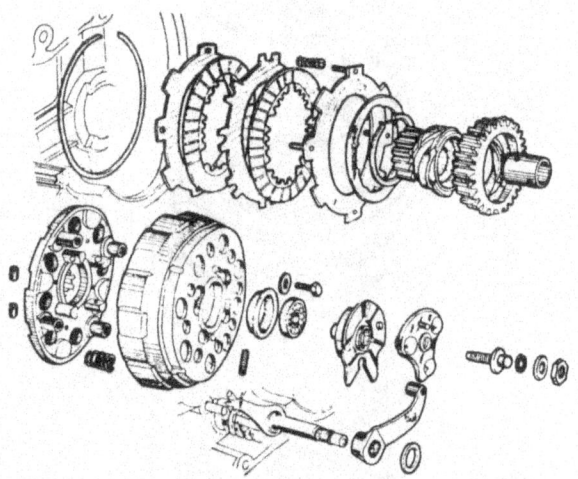

FIG. 11. THE HONDA AUTOMATIC CLUTCH DESIGN

Employed on the C.100, C.102, C.105E and "Monkey Bike" models this clutch is operated by centrifugal force, yet also incorporates a two-way positive control to ensure easy gear changing and kick starting.

merely freewheels on the gearbox shaft. The clutch centre is fixed to the gearbox shaft, but is not connected to the primary drive. It is the job of the plates to form a link between the two. Strong springs hold the lined and unlined plates together. When the clutch is home, the friction between the driving and driven plates is such that they revolve together. The drive therefore reaches the gearbox through the combined motion of the clutch body and centre, transmitted through the plates.

When the clutch is operated the pressure on the springs is relieved and there is insufficient friction between the plates to enable any movement to be transmitted. Instead the plates which are splined to the clutch centre merely remain stationary while the adjacent plates which are splined to the clutch body freewheel. Gradual release of the clutch lever brings the plates together progressively, and the drive is therefore taken up smoothly. This happens whenever the machine is moved away from a standstill.

When changing gear freeing the clutch momentarily relieves the gears of loading and enables them to move easily.

On the C.100 and C.102 scooterettes the clutch is controlled centrifugally, and is also coupled so that it disengages momentarily as the footchange pedal is operated.

THE CYCLE PARTS

When a motor-cycle is driven along a road it remains upright for exactly the same reason that a gyroscope refuses to topple over—its two revolving wheels act, in effect, as a pair of gyroscopes, and resist attempts to force them out of their course.

There are, however, other factors which enter into it. One is the design of the steering gear. This is so arranged that, although the fact is not immediately apparent, the front wheel is trailing, rather like the castor of an armchair. To some extent the steering characteristics depend upon the amount of trail specified by the designer, and upon certain other factors such as the rake of the steering head, the weight distribution of the machine, and the correlation of the centre of gravity with the roll centre. And, of course, the efficiency or otherwise of the suspension systems plays a considerable part. With the exception of CB.72/77 Super Sports, all the Honda machines use a leading-link front fork which gives the minimum of wheel-base variation. In the 250 c.c. Dream the links are joined together to form a U-shaped arm and so relieve the front spindle of the work involved in stiffening a pair of links. The CB.72 and CB.77 use a telescopic fork, chosen for its combination of sensitivity and direct action.

At the rear all Hondas use a swinging-fork layout controlled by two spring units. Hydraulic damping is employed at both front and rear. This is designed to eliminate oscillation which would otherwise result from the action of the suspension springs. A hydraulic damper consists of an oil chamber formed in one of the two members of the telescopic unit and a disc valve carried on the other. On a bump the oil is forced past the valve and offers little or no resistance to movement. On the return stroke, however, the action of the valve is such that the oil has to pass back through restricted channels in the piston of which the valve is part. The resulting drag slows down the rebound action of the forks.

BRAKES

Just as important as making a motor-cycle go is the ability to make it stop. On the Honda this is the job of a pair of internal-expanding brakes. On the 50 c.c. models, and the C.92 and C.72 machines both front and rear brakes are of leading-and-trailing shoe internal-expanding type. In these, a pair of shoes, carrying friction linings, is arranged concentrically inside the brake drum. One end of each shoe rests on a common pivot, and interposed between the other ends is a cam, operated through an arm by movement of the brake lever or pedal.

When the brake is applied the arm rotates the cam, which forces the shoes apart until their friction linings meet the drum. The resistance which they offer to rotation absorbs energy, and the machine stops. As the shoes are spring-loaded together, releasing the brake causes them to snap back into position.

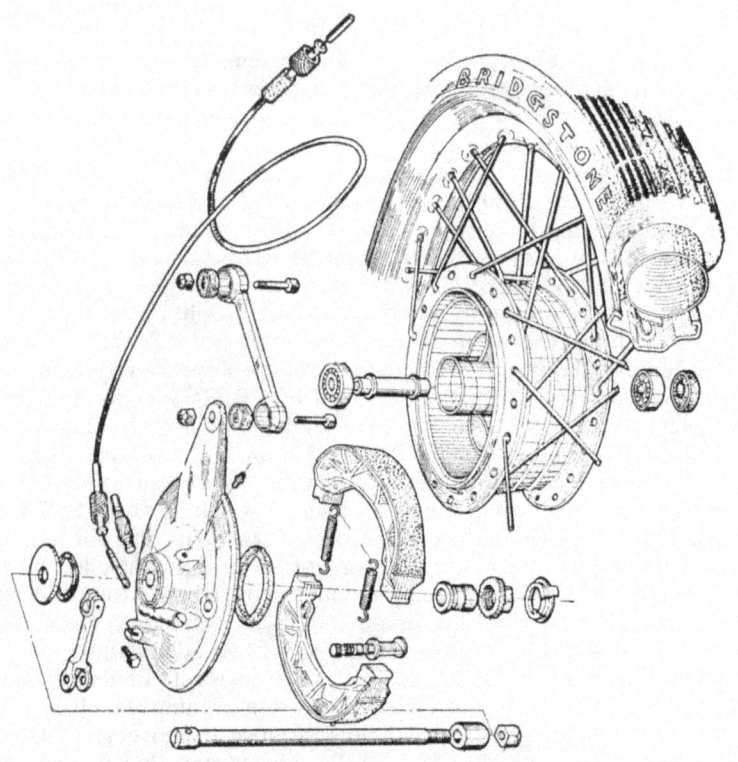

FIG. 12. INSIDE A HONDA FRONT BRAKE
Seen in exploded form, this internal-expanding brake is the type fitted to the C.110 and C.114 machines. A torque arm anchors the plate.

On the sports models, a two-leading-shoe brake is used at the front. On a brake of this type each shoe rests on its own pivot, placed at opposite sides of the back plate. Each shoe has its own cam, interconnected through a rod linkage. Operation of brake control causes the leading edge of each shoe to move outwards and come into contact with the drum. Since the leading edge is, initially, the more effective part of the shoe the result is greater immediate braking force.

CHAPTER IV

FAULT TRACING

WHEN a doctor wishes to diagnose a patient's illness he works methodically, listing the various symptoms to build up an overall picture of the complaint. Then, with the help of his knowledge of the way the body works, he can identify the illness and give the appropriate treatment.

Exactly the same procedure has to be followed when a motor-cycle refuses to work. Obviously there is a fault—some reason why it won't work—and before the fault can be cured it has got to be located and identified. The search has to be just as methodical in its way as is the doctor's.

Take the engine first. Assuming that certain basic requirements are met the engine *must* work. If it is not working it is proof that one or more of these requirements are not being met, and fault tracing is discovering which and why.

An engine must work if the correct charge of petrol/air mixture is being induced into the cylinder at the right time and is properly compressed and fired by a spark occurring at the right time, and the residue properly exhausted.

The first stage must be the obvious one of checking that there is, in fact, a supply of petrol reaching the carburettor. The first thing to do—surprisingly very often overlooked—is to remove the tank cap and make sure that there is some petrol. That done, and assuming that there is ample fuel, check that the petrol tap is switched on. If the supply is low, switch over to the reserve position (on those models which are equipped with reserve taps).

Taking the check one stage further, depress the carburettor tickler and hold it down until fuel floods out of the overflow pipe. If none appears by the time ten seconds have elapsed it is a pretty clear indication that the tap or the fuel line is blocked, or the needle valve in the float chamber is jammed. To locate the seat of the trouble switch off the fuel, detach the fuel pipe at the float chamber end, and switch on again, when fuel should flow freely from the pipe. If it doesn't then obviously the blockage is in the pipe or the tap. Switch off once more, detach the pipe completely, then switch on again. If fuel flows through the tap then the pipe is the culprit—and that should be easy to clear. But if there is no fuel flow then your trouble is in the tap, and it will need to be stripped for cleaning.

Should your first check on the fuel lines indicate that petrol is reaching the end of the pipe but not entering the carburettor it shows quite clearly that the fault lies in the float mechanism. The remedy is to remove the carburettor float bowl, again switch on the petrol, and watch the action of the float-controlled needle-valve. Frequently, working the valve with the fingers will free whatever obstruction had caused the blockage, and the flow of petrol which follows will then be sufficient to flush the valve. In obstinate cases the only solution is to remove the valve and wash it in petrol. If the needle shows signs of damage replace the valve assembly with a new one.

It is possible for the fuel system to be at fault by supplying too much fuel, as well as by supplying too little. Overflooding, as this type of

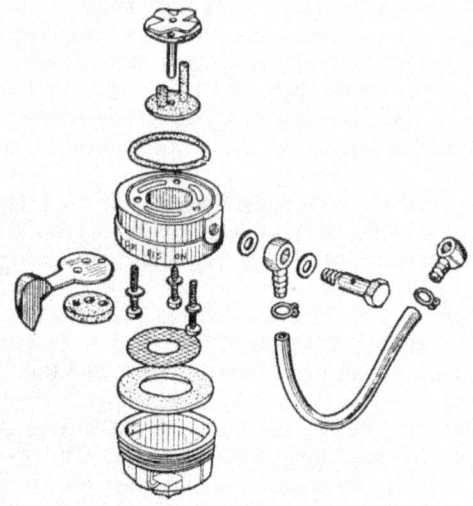

FIG. 13. A FUEL TAP WITH INTEGRAL FILTER

trouble is called, is depressingly easy to recognize—fuel pours from the overflow pipe whenever the tap is switched on and the engine, if it runs at all, constantly misfires and has a lumpy exhaust note.

Only the float assembly can be responsible for this particular form of trouble. A float may be punctured, in which case it sinks to the bottom of the chamber and allows the valve to remain almost fully open. But it is more likely that the answer is that dirt has entered the needle valve and is holding it off its seating. Even a tiny speck of hard matter is sufficient to prevent the needle from seating properly, and there is thus a constant trickle of fuel into the chamber. The effects of this milder form of overflooding would be more noticeable at the lower engine speeds, when the excess fuel cannot be used up quickly enough. At high speeds the unit tends to take all the fuel it can get fairly happily, providing the critical petrol/air ratio of 12:1 (which gives maximum power) is not exceeded.

Besides a punctured float and dirt, it is also possible for overflooding to be caused by a bent float needle or by pitted faces on the needle and its tapered seating. This latter fault, however, is unlikely to be met until a carburettor has had many thousands of miles of use.

Akin to overflooding in its effects on the running of the engine is an incorrect petrol level in the float chamber. This is caused by the setting of the float having been deranged, so that the petrol level has to be higher before the needle will be pushed home. In all these cases stripping the system and examining and checking the components should uncover the fault.

Where initial inspection of the fuel system shows no immediately obvious fault the next stage of the fault tracing should be switched to the ignition system, and especially to the sparking plug. To a knowledgeable rider the plug can often tell a great deal about the conditions inside the engine. If the plug points and insulator are covered with soft black soot it is positive proof that the engine is running over-rich. On the other hand, if these parts have an ash-white appearance the inference is that the mixture is extremely weak, and one can begin to think in terms of blocked jets, or some other form of fuel starvation. Hard carbon on the plug shows that oil is being burned inside the cylinders—a sign of worn bores, or perhaps of faulty rings. But a plug which is coloured a deep coffee shade indicates that the mixture and combustion are normal.

Examination of the plug will thus give a good general guide to the engine's internal health and may offer some valuable clue which will enable you to trace the cause of the breakdown. But don't be misled into allowing the plug itself to escape untested. To do this, leave the plug connected to the H.T. lead. Switch on the ignition, and then ground the plug body against a clean part of the cylinder so that there is an adequate earth. Angle the plug so that you can see the points gap clearly (first checking that the gap is as specified), and then operate the starter. A fat blue spark should jump across the gap. Repeat this test several times. You should get the same result on each occasion.

If there is no spark you have a fault somewhere in the ignition system and your next step is to find out exactly where it is. First of all, eliminate the plug from your list of suspects by substituting for it a brand-new plug. Or if the motor-cycle is a "twin" and the second cylinder has been working normally take the plug out of that and use it for your elimination check.

Whichever you use—new plug or proved plug—repeat the test just described. If there is a good spark to reward you then the obvious inference is that the old plug's insulation had broken down and the current was shorting straight to earth instead of jumping the points. Fitting a new plug in its place (after checking the gap) should thus completely cure the trouble. But if, on the other hand, the new plug fails as well then the fault lies somewhere between the plug terminal and the current source, and a much more exhaustive check will be needed.

Start with the plug cap. For a satisfactory test you will need a long pin or a nail or a piece of wire. Detach the plug cap—it screws into the lead—and into the hole bored by its screw threads thrust the pin. Then, with the ignition on, hold the lead by the insulated section so that the pin is about an eighth of an inch from the cylinder head and operate the starter. If a spark jumps from the pin to the head it proves that current is reaching the end of the H.T. lead but is not passing through the cap and into the central electrode of the plug. Snipping a quarter of an inch or so off the lead so that the cap screw bites into fresh cable may cure the trouble. If not, a new cap will be required.

Where no current is flowing in the H.T. lead turn your attention to the wiring. Check all contacts and all low-tension wires for security, and make sure that the H.T. lead's insulation is undamaged. Try the effect of wiring in a fresh length of H.T. lead temporarily. If this works it is proof that the old lead has been fractured or earthed.

Using the wiring diagram as a guide, trace the wires from the ignition switch. The action of the switch itself is plainly visible from the operation or otherwise of the neutral lamp when the ignition is on and the gear is in the neutral position—if the lamp lights then the switch circuit is obviously in order. Lastly, examine the contact-breaker points and check the gap between them. If the points are dirty give them a clean and then try the ignition again. A roadside clean-up which is adequate for the purpose can be made by inserting a piece of stiff clean card between the points, closing them gently on it, and sliding it out against slight resistance from the contacts. Repeated half a dozen times this will remove surface contamination. Check the gaps too, and rectify them if they are too wide or too narrow. Signs of severe burning of the points is evidence that the condenser has failed.

If all these checks still produce no reason why the ignition system should be inoperative the probability is that a major failure has occurred, and that the job will have to be referred to an agent who has special equipment for checking circuitry.

Complete engine failure for any reason other than ignition or fuel trouble is unlikely, save in the somewhat remote event of such a vital part as the cam chain snapping. Other troubles are far more likely to show themselves in reduced performance or erratic running.

One of the likelier causes of lack of pulling power is an incorrect tappet setting—and on Hondas the tappet clearances are very critical indeed. There is a good reason for clearance being allowed between the tappet and the valve stem. It enables the expansion of the engine when warm to be taken up. If the tappet was tight when the unit was cold the expansion of the parts would result in the valve being held away from its seating. The efficiency of the cylinder would thus be badly impaired for compression would be lowered, the working pressures reduced, and the valve seats would be exposed to the searing flame of the burning charge and would quickly deteriorate.

Where tight tappets are suspected it is possible to deduce where the fault lies by the way the engine behaves. If it is an inlet valve which is not being properly closed there will be a tendency for the engine to spit back through the carburettor, since some mixture will be driven back during the compression stroke and there will also be a leakage of gas during the power stroke. Where it is an exhaust valve which is not seating properly the mixture tends to be driven into the exhaust system and ignite there prematurely by virtue of its contact with the hot pipe. This gives rise to banging and rumbling in the exhaust. In both cases the affected cylinder tends to run hot, and if the trouble is really severe it may cut out altogether at low speeds. The plug will of course reflect the trouble accurately enough on the inspection which should be done as a matter of course, but with the twins it is possible to isolate the faulty cylinder by the very simple expedient of setting the engine to a fast tick-over and detaching each plug lead in turn. When the lead is taken off the cylinder which is *not* developing its full power the engine speed will fall only slightly. When the lead is removed from the cylinder which is pulling its weight there will be a marked drop in engine speed and the unit will probably stop completely. In cases of doubt it is better to err on the safe side and make a check on *all* the tappets. It is impossible to set them accurately with the engine hot, and most inadvisable to run with a tight tappet. As an emergency measure any tappet which is found to be tight when the piston is at top dead centre on the compression stroke should be slackenened off until there is either no up and down play at all, or else just a barely perceptible amount of play. This is purely a "get you home" measure. When the engine is stone cold the tappets must be readjusted to the correct gap in the normal way.

Loss of compression can be caused in several other ways. If the unit has been run for any length of time when suffering from chronic overheating there is always a possibility that the cylinder head/cylinder block joint may have become distorted. In such cases, there will probably be a distinct hiss as gas escapes from the fractured joint on compression and exhaust strokes—or even an ominous cracking sound as hot gases bite their way out whenever the engine fires. Damage such as this calls for workshop treatment, since the head will need to be checked and refaced. Remedial measures should be taken as soon as possible because such a condition is one which gets worse the longer it is left. The reason is not far to seek. The leaking joint lowers the efficiency of the engine and allows air to dilute the mixture. This, in turn, leads to more overheating, which causes worse distortion.

Though the Honda engine is a sturdy and long-suffering unit it is utterly dependent upon regular oil changes, and these should not be delayed or neglected. With use oils tend to lose much of their lubricating properties, and if a seizure should occur there is always a danger that the piston rings may be fractured. Besides losing compression the engine would then immediately start to burn oil, causing the exhaust system to smoke heavily. If ever this should happen, stop immediately—for the rings must almost certainly be broken and any further running will cause heavy scoring of the bores. The broken ends of piston rings make highly efficient cutting tools when propelled at internal-combustion engine speeds, so the cylinder could be virtually ruined.

Transmission faults are far more straightforward—either the drive is being transmitted properly or it isn't. But just occasionally what may seem to be a mild loss of power could be the beginnings of clutch slip, and where no apparent fault can be found in the engine it is always advisable to check on the adjustment and the condition of the clutch. Slip will be at its most noticeable if the throttle is opened sharply in the low gear on a stiff gradient. If the engine revs rise with no corresponding immediate improvement in traction it is a sure sign that the clutch is slipping, either through maladjustment or because the plates are wearing thin. No other cause is likely.

The process of elimination can also be employed successfully to isolate faults in the lighting system, bearing in mind the fact that if electricity is present and the circuit is complete then the electricity *must* flow. Where a circuit is dead it can be for only one of two reasons—either there is no electricity there, or else the circuit is wrong.

Faulty circuits are of two types—the open circuit and the short circuit. In the first case there is a simple break in the wiring. To use the railway analogy again, there is a rail missing. The train (our electricity) can therefore come up the line only as far as that point, and then halt. To get the train moving again it is necessary to repair the line. Electrically speaking, the whole of the wire from the current source to the break is still live but beyond the break it is dead.

The short circuit, on the other hand, can be regarded as a bit of faulty points-setting. Instead of the train being directed on to the correct line the signalman has diverted it on to a loop which leads back to the terminal. The train can continue to circulate on this loop line indefinitely, but it cannot take the right track until the points have been reset to allow it to do so.

As with the train, so with the electricity. Instead of a simple fracture of the wire we have a live conductor which has come into electrical contact with some uninsulated part of the machine. Since electricity invariably takes the shortest path to earth, our current has gone rushing off on this more attractive shorter route. In this case there is still a fully live circuit, but it is the wrong one! The useful part—the one that leads to one of the machine's components—is dead.

Before one can trace a circuit it is essential to have the appropriate wiring diagram and to be able to read it. At first sight this is a depressing prospect, for the average wiring diagram seems more like a small-scale plan of Hampton Court Maze. However, with practice it is possible to

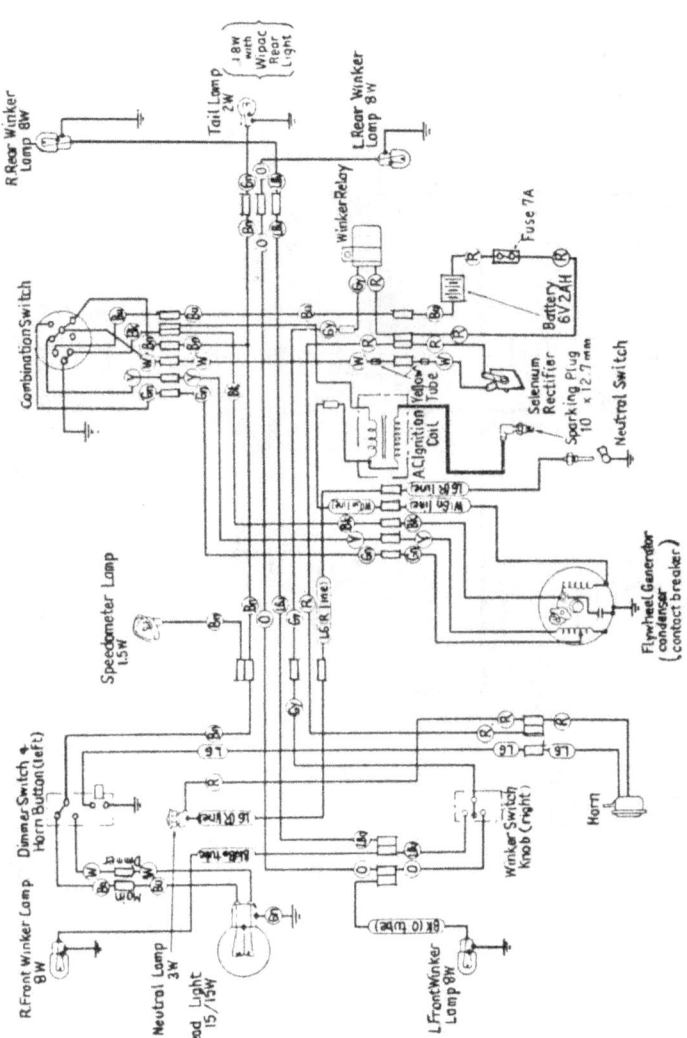

Fig. 14. Wiring Diagram, Honda C.100

Bk = black. Bu = blue. Bn = brown. Gy = grey. Gn = green. L.Bu = light blue. LG = light green. O = orange. R = red. W = white. Y = yellow. Bu-tube = sheathed in light blue plastics. O-tube = sheathed in orange plastics. R-line = red line. Gn-line = green line.

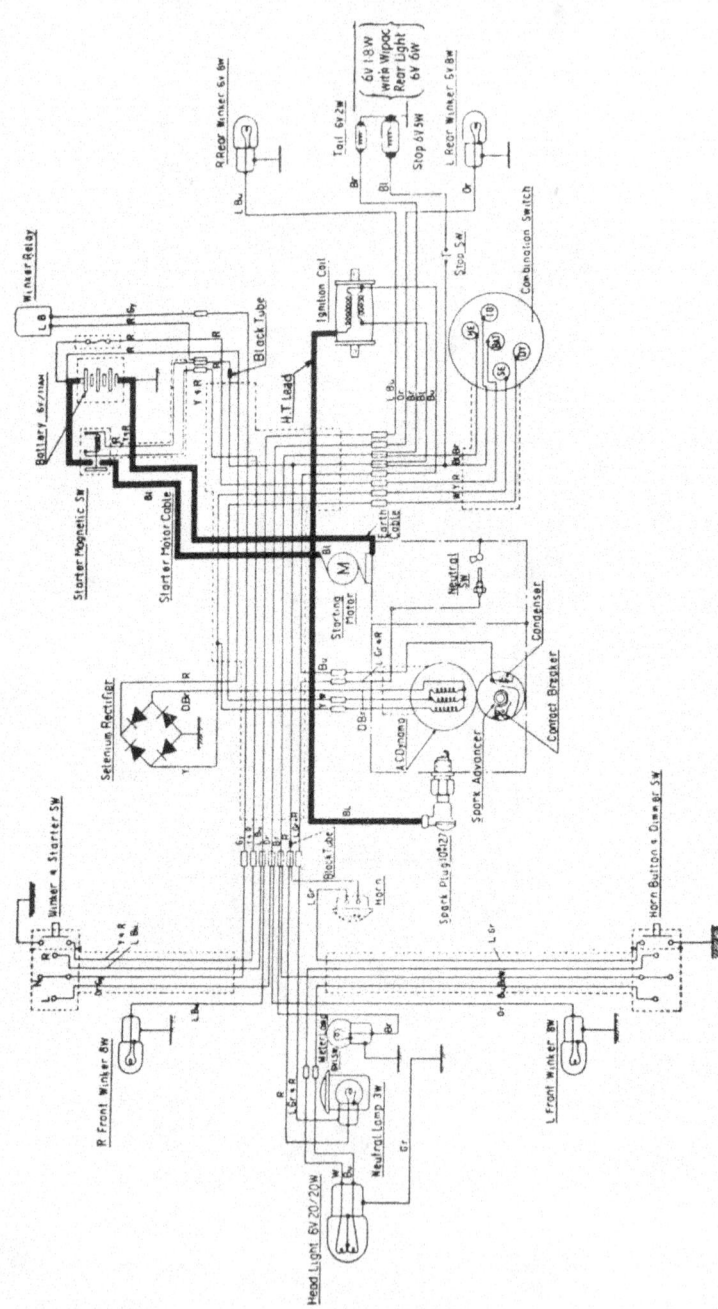

FIG. 15.—WIRING DIAGRAM, HONDA C.102

For abbreviations see Fig. 14—wiring diagram of Model C.100—which is similar, save for the use of a starter motor on the Model C.102.

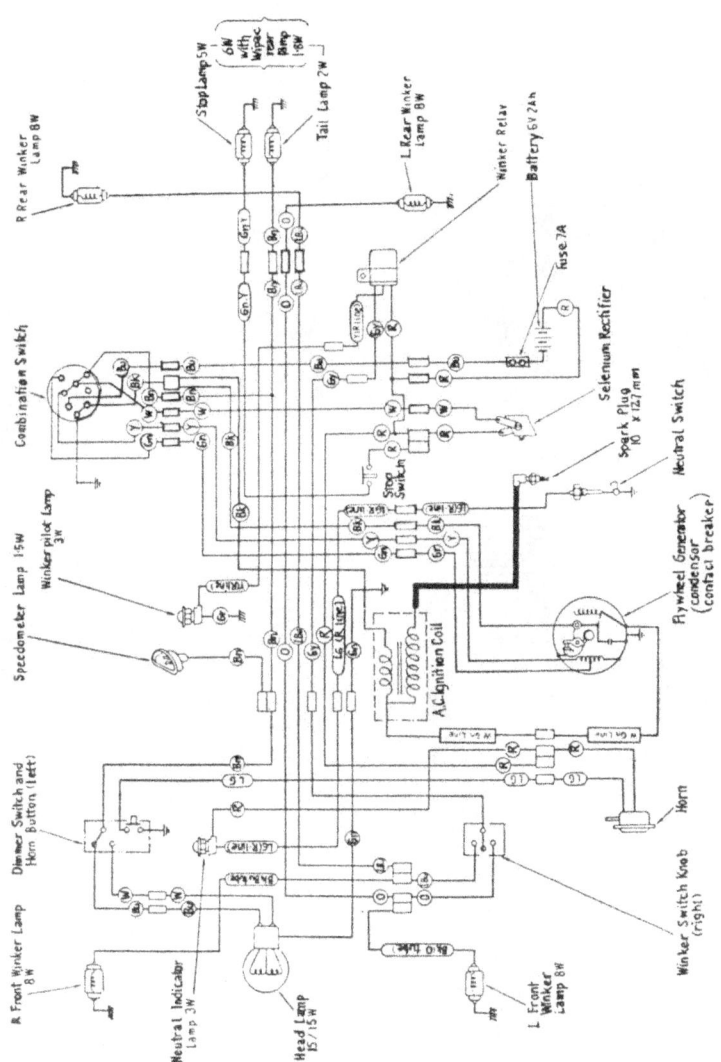

FIG. 16. WIRING DIAGRAM, MODELS C.110 AND C.114
For abbreviations see Fig. 14—wiring diagram of the Model C.100.

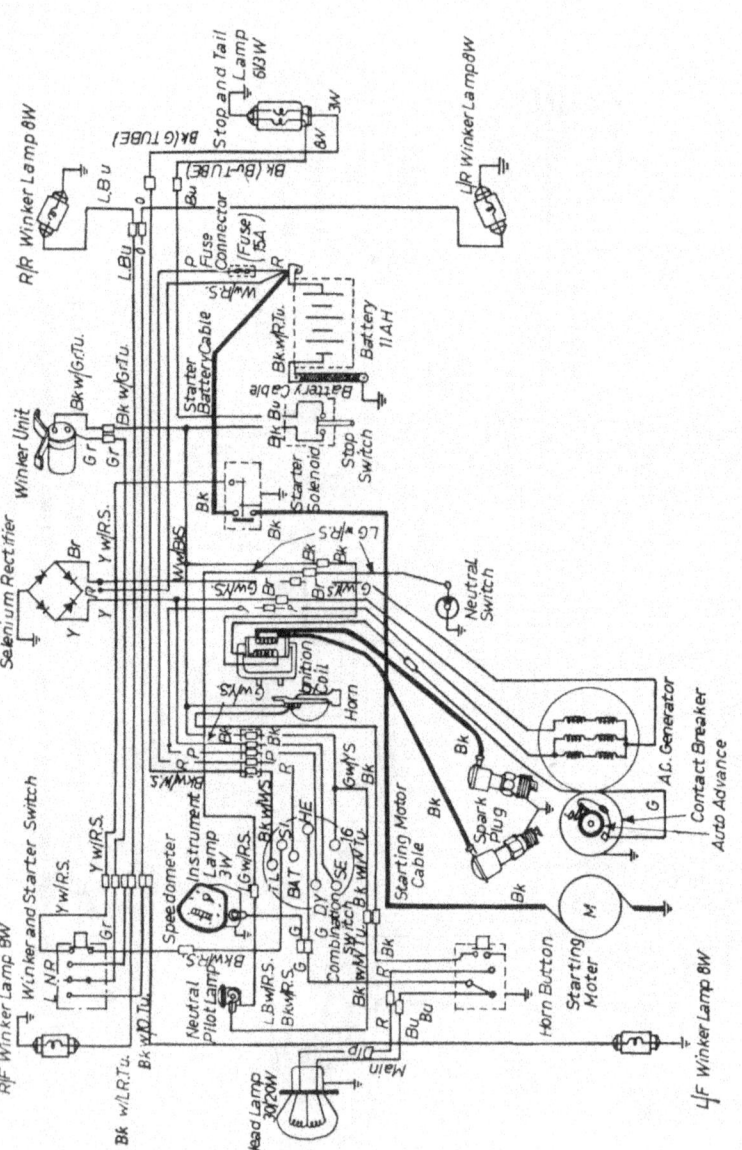

Fig. 17. Wiring Diagram, Model C.92 Twin

Bk = black. Br = brown. Bu = blue. G = green. R = red. Y = yellow. P = pink. Bk.w/RS = black, red spiral. Bk.w/WS = black, white spiral. W.w/RS = white, red spiral. Y.w/RS = yellow, red spiral. Bk.w/LB Tu. = black, light blue sheath. Bk.w/O.tu = black, orange sheath. Bk.w/W.Tu. = black, white sheath. Bk.w/Gr.Tu. = black, grey sheath.

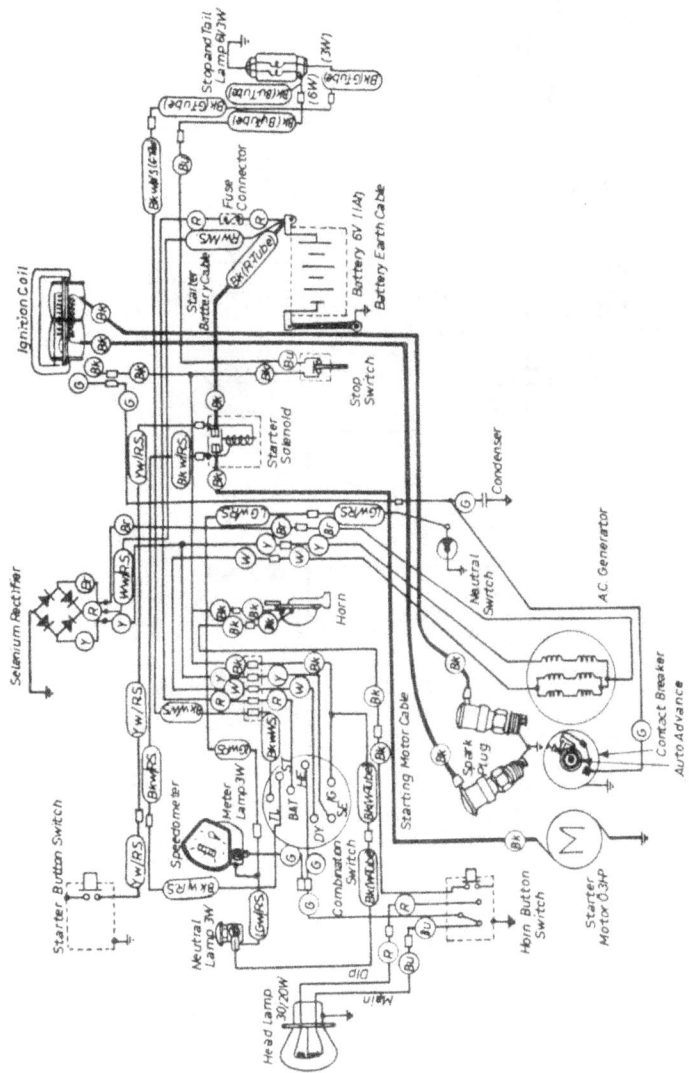

FIG. 18. WIRING DIAGRAM, MODEL CB.92 TWIN
For abbreviations see Fig. 17—wiring diagram for Model C.92 twin.

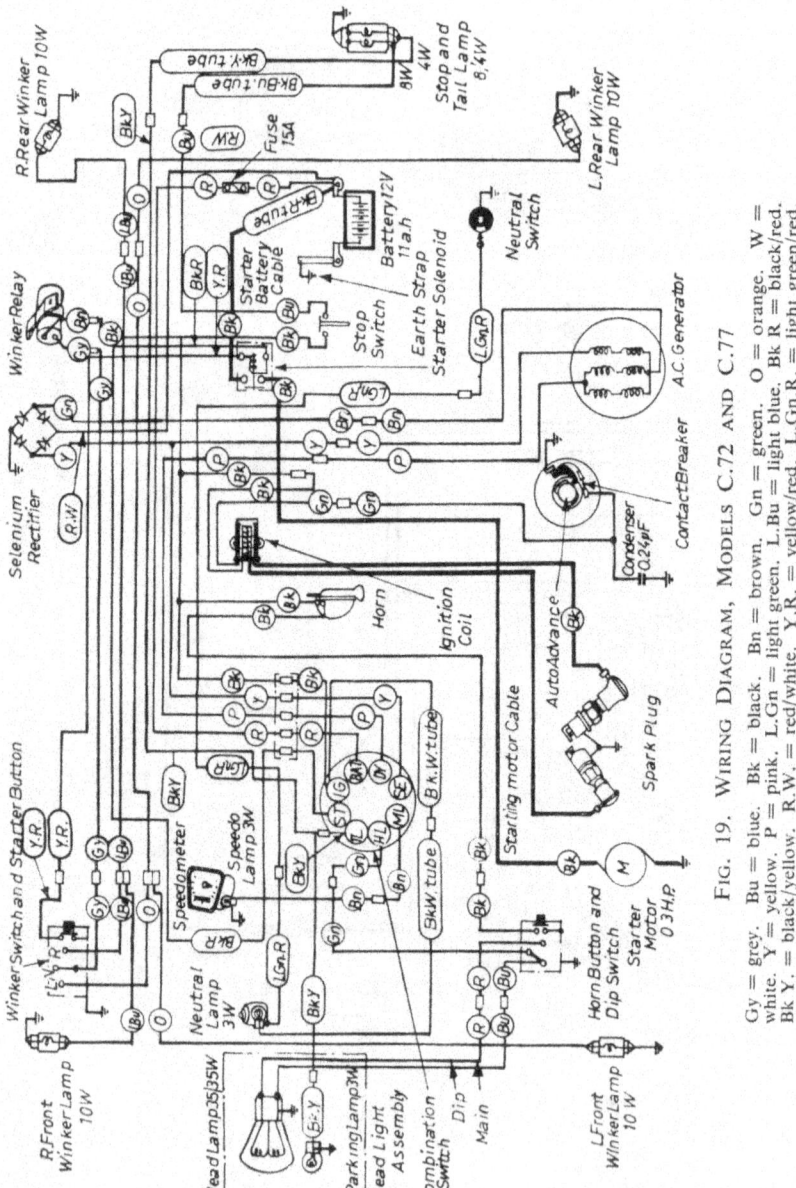

Fig. 19. Wiring Diagram, Models C.72 and C.77

Gy = grey. Bu = blue. Bk = black. Bn = brown. Gn = green. O = orange. W = white. Y = yellow. P = pink. L.Gn = light green. L.Bu = light blue. Bk R = black/red. Bk Y. = black/yellow. R.W. = red/white. Y.R. = yellow/red. L.Gn.R. = light green/red. Bk Y. tube = black, yellow sheath. Bk Bu tube = black, blue sheath. Bk R. tube = red sheath. Bk W. tube = black, white sheath.

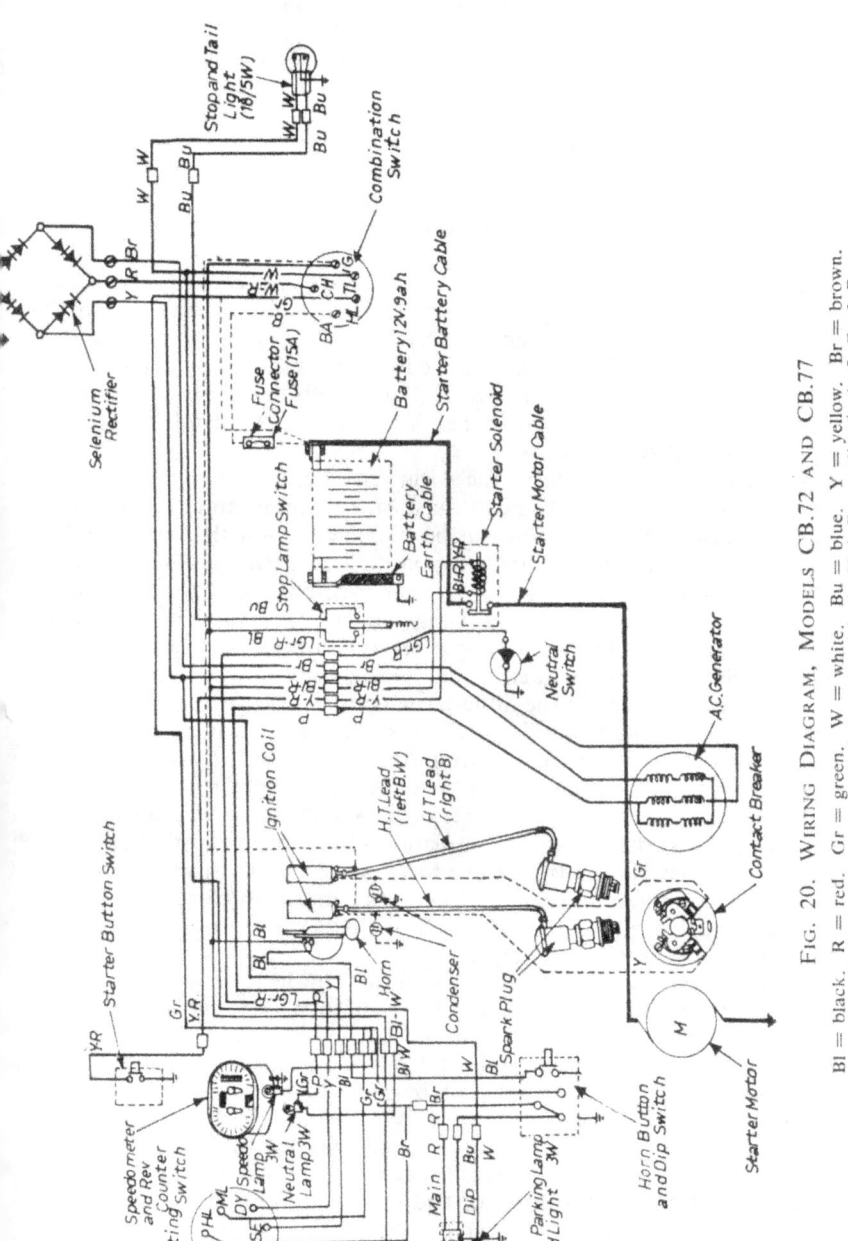

FIG. 20. WIRING DIAGRAM, MODELS CB.72 AND CB.77

Bl = black. R = red. Gr = green. W = white. Bu = blue. Y = yellow. Br = brown. P = pink. L.Gr = light green. Bl & R = black/red. Y & R = yellow/red. L.Gr & R = light green/red. W & R = white/red. Bl & W = black/white. Solid lines, harness "B." Dotted lines, harness "A."

follow the circuits very accurately—providing the word circuit is always borne in mind. Part of the confusion arises from the fact that it is only the outward path of the current which appears on the diagram. The return is invariably through earth—which in this instance means the frame of the machine. Any components which are earthed to the frame are, therefore, automatically connected to one another electrically.

Where specific circuits have to be checked it is a good plan to obtain a sharp pencil and a piece of tracing paper and trace just that one circuit. With this data in your hand go to the machine and check through the various leads stage by stage. It helps to have a circuit tester—a small sharp pointer with a neon bulb in its handle and a clip by which it can be attached to the machine. Earth the clip, and press the pointer into the wire or on to contacts at intervals. If the bulb lights there is current flowing. If it doesn't, there is none. With the aid of such a tool circuit testing becomes relatively easy.

When the faulty section of the wiring has been located it should be closely examined so that the exact cause of the failure can be determined. A break inside the insulation can be pinpointed with the tester, or by simply tugging in opposite directions on the lead until you find a spot at which the casing merely stretches. This is where the lead has broken.

Where the suspect lead is a very long one, or is inaccessible, an alternative method of checking is to by-pass it with a long test lead equipped with small crocodile clips at each end. One is connected to each terminal and the circuit tested. If the hitherto inoperative component then works it shows that the fault is in the lead. In some cases it may be possible to draw a new lead into place by wiring it to the old one and then pulling it through from the far end, using the old lead as a guide.

To repair fractured leads so that no undue electrical stresses are set up the joint and the subsequent insulation should be made good as carefully as possible. If it is practicable to solder on proper snap connectors and encase them in an insulated sleeve this is much to be preferred. At the least the new joint should be well twisted together and bound over with two layers of insulating tape.

Terminals which have been undone must be properly retightened, and any new connectors crimped or soldered into place. Otherwise, high resistances and consequent early failure may ensue. Soldered joints are always preferred to plain ones, except in the case of the bared ends of wires clamped into a terminal post by means of a grub screw. Here binding the ends of the wire with solder is inadvisable since the grub screw may work loose in the resulting hollow and thus give erratic contact.

If these points are borne in mind there is no reason why the average owner should not be able to trace and rectify most minor faults on his machine, and provide at least a temporary cure.

CHAPTER V

TOOLS

NOBODY could make a bigger mistake than to embark on serious maintenance work without an adequate set of tools—especially on a piece of engineering made with the precision of a Honda. True, Honda excel most other makes in the size and the quality of the tool kit supplied with the machine. Even so this is intended more for running repairs and simple routine maintenance than as a comprehensive kit to enable you to strip your motor-cycle, and for some jobs special tools are advised. This is not because the manufacturer thinks he can make a good thing out of selling them—in fact special tools are normally pretty uneconomic from his point of view—but because the machines are built to such fine engineering limits that this equipment is essential if parts are to be removed without damage.

Even where the jobs which are to be tackled do not call for special tools they still require the use of good tools. Cheap tools are a bad investment. Not only do they wear out quickly but they also have an infuriating habit of ruining nut and bolt heads as they do so. If you intend to become a *real* rider-mechanic get yourself a tool kit which will also play its part. A set of good metric chrome-vanadium open-enders is essential. They are sold in sets containing half a dozen spanners, and these will give you an ample range of jaw sizes. Complement these with a set of metric ring spanners—although these are not as handy as are open-enders when you have to get them into confined spaces, they have the outstanding advantage of being unable to slip off a nut.

A socket set can be regarded as a luxury—though if you ride a Honda, you will probably think, as I do, that such a magnificent machine deserves the best in the way of tools to go with it. And there is no doubt that a comprehensive socket set *is* the best, even though it cannot wholly replace either open-ended or ring spanners. Used with a variety of extension bars, however, sockets are both versatile and a hundred per cent safe. You can even obtain a universally-jointed extension which will enable the sockets to be used round corners, and it is possible to obtain such desirable extras as ratchet or torque wrenches to go with them. For the average rider, however, a good stout set of box spanners will probably fill the bill almost as well. Made of steel tubing, box spanners can exert a considerable force if used with a sturdy tommy bar. It is essential, however, to buy only well-known brands, for cheap box spanners soon revert to being mere tubes!

Your tool kit already contains a choice of screwdrivers, but it is no bad plan to equip yourself with a pair of electrical screwdrivers for specialist electrical work—one of them short-bladed, the other with a long, partly insulated blade. For this, too, a pair of pliers incorporating wire cutters and strippers is essential. You will also need a set of feeler gauges, a collection of tin boxes with lids for the storage of small parts which are removed during overhauls, a valve spring compressor, and a grease gun. This last-named should be of the high-pressure type which can develop terrific pressures—over 8,000 p.s.i. have been recorded.

Make sure that you have proper surroundings in which to work. A machine as intricate as the Honda cannot be stripped in a road or a passageway. You need working space and plenty of light. An adjustable lamp, or one of the cheap clip-on lead lamps, will be helpful.

USING YOUR TOOLS

There is far more to the use of even the simplest of hand tools than merely placing them into position and tugging hard till the nut frees. Each particular type of spanner has its own characteristics and, generally speaking, for any one job you will find there is one type of spanner better suited for it than any other.

Unquestionably the great all-rounders of the tool kit are the open-enders which are slimly built and can, therefore, be slipped into confined spaces which no other spanner could reach. You will notice that their jaws are angled. This means that the open-ender will successfully loosen a nut even when you cannot obtain sufficient purchase to make more than a few degrees turn at a time. When the limit of movement has been reached it is possible simply to reverse the spanner and so obtain room in which to turn the nut a little more. In this way it is possible to undo a recalcitrant nut by easy stages.

It is, of course, essential that only the right size of spanner should be used. The open-ender is designed to apply its pressure along the flats of a nut or bolt and is consequently made with jaws of just the right width to grip them. If too large a spanner is used the jaws will press against the angles instead of on the flats, when one of two things can then happen. Either the spanner will gouge away the angles to leave a useless rounded head, or else the bolt head will prevail and spring open the jaws of the spanner. In the first case no spanner will in future be of the slightest use on that hexagon; in the second the spanner itself becomes just so much scrap.

Damage to the jaws can also be caused by applying excessive force when trying to free a bolt which refuses to budge. There is always a temptation to deal with the stubborn thing by slipping a piece of piping over the spanner to increase the leverage, or by locking the jaws of a pair of spanners together. The best advice is—don't. Sometimes these methods will succeed, but normally you will only apply excessive force and ruin the spanner. And there is always a danger of breaking the bolt completely.

Here is where socket, ring, or box spanners come into their own. Rings and sockets do not grip on the flats of the head but on the angles, and consequently force is applied all the way round. Boxes bear both on flats and angles. Obviously they have the advantage over spanners which can grip only on two surfaces. Consequently the same hand pressure applied through a ring or socket as was exerted through an open-ender will often free a nut which had previously resisted. Box spanners may, however, not prove quite so successful since the tommy bar may bend and unless a considerable downward force is applied the box may also tend to ride off the nut.

When using a spanner to tighten nuts and bolts it is important to remember that excessive force should not be employed. Spanners are designed to exert just sufficient force with hand pressure to tighten up most nuts and bolts correctly, and if excessive force is used the result may be to snap the bolt completely. At best the threads may be seriously strained. An exception is made only when definite instructions are given by the manufacturer—usually in the form of torque settings.

It is particularly important to bear this in mind on a machine such as the Honda in which a considerable amount of light alloy is used. The steel bolt is so much harder than the material into which it is threaded and over-enthusiasm with the spanner will merely rip the threads inside the hole and the bolt will come out.

Pliers, of course, should never be used as makeshift spanners since the jaws can never be parallel and the serrated pipe grip is perilously liable to slip. A rounded hexagon is the inevitable result if it does.

Neither should adjustable spanners be used, save in an absolute emergency. Here again it is impossible to set the jaws to the required accuracy, and rounded hexagons result.

Screwdrivers must have their blades properly ground so that, in side view, the blade is at first concave and then runs parallel as far as the tip. This enables it to be seated properly in the slot, and the pressure it applies is then equally distributed along the slot sides. A screwdriver with a wedge-shaped blade in side view does not seat properly and instead of an even pressure all the force is concentrated on the edges of the slot. These crumble and the screw is ruined. For cross-headed screws use only cross-headed screwdrivers. These come in two sizes and in two grades of hardness. Stick to those supplied in the Honda tool kit and you will be on the safe side.

After use, all tools should be wiped clean. They should be kept lightly oiled if they are used infrequently, and in any case wrap them in clean and dry rag (*not* plastics as these cause condensation and lead to rust). Before using them again, wipe off the oil film or the tools may slip when any pressure is applied.

CHAPTER VI

GENERAL MAINTENANCE

JUST as, in everyday life, it is more important to keep fit than to be forever undergoing medical treatment and enduring major surgery, so with a Honda it is more important to keep it in good running order than to be continually stripping and rebuilding it.

On the face of it this may seem obvious, but a surprisingly large number of owners overlook the point and their engines tend to spend almost as much time in pieces as in action. Small defects neglected inevitably become major defects and these call for a stripdown to rectify the damage, and the stripdown in turn disturbs parts which have become bedded-in and settled. For a while the efficiency of the entire unit suffers.

Given the specified regular maintenance, any one of the Honda models can cover a quite surprising mileage before there is any real need to strip the power unit or even to have the head off for a "decoke." If, however, the routine maintenance is neglected the time which can elapse between overhauls is drastically shortened—and so is the life of the machine. Additionally the amount of work to be done and the amount of money to be spent will increase.

This is because maladjustments tend to have a cumulative effect. The Honda engine is tough—remarkably tough—but it is a piece of precision engineering, too, and it depends on this precision for the excellent performance which it gives. Run it fifty miles or so with a tight exhaust tappet and, though the power will fall off, little harm will be done. But in the absence of a routine check the exact nature of the fault may go undetected for hundreds of miles and all sorts of troubles can then result from this one minor example of neglect. The hot, newly-ignited mixture in the cylinder (and it is hot—exhaust valves work in temperatures up to 600°F) plays on the narrow sealing areas of the valve and seat like a blow-torch, scorching and pitting the metal. The stem of the valve may also be damaged. Since there is then leakage on compression and on firing the engine cannot develop its designed power and so the speed and acceleration power drop while fuel consumption rises. Eventually nothing but lifting the head and fitting a new valve will make good the damage. And that's a pretty stiff price to pay for the minute or so saved by not carrying out a weekly tappet check.

It is not only engines which can suffer in this way. The brakes are an even more glaring example. So good are the anchors on the Hondas that there is a considerable temptation to use them and forget them. They will, it is true, go on working for months with no apparent deterioration. But they *do* deteriorate—so gradually that the rider just doesn't notice that it's happening. He adjusts himself to the slowly altering feel and to the decreasing effectiveness and never for a moment suspects that they are not pulling him up as quickly as they could some months before. It is not till an emergency arises—one which could have been avoided easily

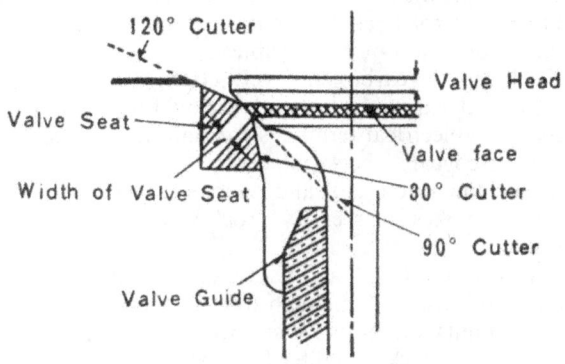

FIG. 21. VALVE SEAT DETAIL

The seating area of the valves is relatively small, as this C.92 diagram shows. Where grinding will not suffice, damaged seats must be recut.

if the brakes were in good order—that the real truth dawns. It can be a dangerous, if effective, lesson. And, again, it is one which can be avoided merely by testing and adjusting the brakes at regular intervals. Constant and methodical inspection is the best way of preventing any such troubles. Normally, checks and adjustments are recommended on the basis of elapsed mileage. This is an excellent scheme—*if* you keep a detailed log book. But all too often it is done on a basis of chance recollection—and memory is notoriously unreliable.

TASK SYSTEMS

Task systems are fundamentally different. They were devised for the Forces so that vehicles were kept under a constant mechanical check and so that no fault could go undiscovered for significant periods.

Systems suitable for the Hondas can be used on daily or weekly checks. Which is used depends entirely upon the work to which the machine is being put. If, on average, you are covering a couple of hundred miles in a week then the daily system is to be preferred. On the other hand, if your Honda is used mainly for weekend excursions giving a weekly mileage of less than 150 then tasks on a weekly basis can be substituted.

Taking the daily system first, here are Task Lists for all Honda machines. They are designed to cover all major components, yet to carry out these recommendations should never involve the expenditure of more than 10 minutes in a single day. And in most cases only a couple of minutes will be needed, for the idea is to *check*. Adjustments are carried out only if your examination shows that something is amiss.

Daily Task System

Sunday: check adjustment of front and rear brakes; check freedom of action of brake controls; check security of nuts and bolts in braking system; check lubrication of brake cables and linkages.
Monday: check engine/gearbox oil level; check final drive chain tension.
Tuesday: check all exposed electrical wiring for signs of abrasion or fracture; check all electrical terminals for tightness; check operation of all lamps and switchgear; check battery.
Wednesday: examine tyre treads and remove trapped stones; check tyre pressures; check spokes for security; rock wheels and front fork to test for bearing play.
Thursday: on twins and C.110 and C.114, check clutch cable adjustment; on C.100 and C.102 check that clutch frees properly.
Friday: check all nuts and bolts for security; check operation of throttle and choke controls; check fuel filter for clogging.
Saturday: check adjustment of tappets; check sparking plug gap and condition; check contact-breaker points gap and condition.

Alternative Weekly System

Week 1. Check engine/gearbox oil levels; check tappet adjustment; check sparking plug gap and condition; check contact-breaker points gap and condition.
Week 2. Check brakes for adjustment; check all controls for freedom of action and lubrication; check wheels for security of spokes and play in bearings; examine tyre treads and check tyre pressures; check rear chain adjustment.
Week 3. Examine all electrical leads for signs of abrasion or fracture; check all terminals for security; check battery; check operation of horn, lamps, and switchgear.
Week 4. On twins and C.110 and C.114 check clutch cable for adjustment; on C.100 and C.102 ensure clutch plates are freeing; check fuel filters; check all nuts and bolts for security.

By employing this approach to routine maintenance of your Honda you will ensure that most of the major points are, by the daily system, checked at least once a week. Even allowing for a pretty substantial utilization of the machine this should mean that no fault could go undetected for more than about 300 miles—even if you failed to notice it while riding the machine. And most defects would be discovered almost before they had had time to develop.

The weekly system, obviously, is less foolproof. A month could elapse between a fault developing and its being discovered. Consequently I would not advise this approach unless the average monthly mileage covered is less than 500 miles.

Neither the daily nor the weekly scheme covers such obvious periodic items as oil changes and greasings. These still have to be carried out on an elapsed mileage basis—obviously, since the exhaustion of lubricant is a question of actual use—and once again it is only too easy to forget just when the last change was carried out. Here, a useful aid to memory is to stick to the machine a small piece of coloured tape, on which you write "Next oil change due at x miles." On the scooterettes, this can be stuck under the seat just by the filler cap, so that you see it each time you fill the tank. With the motor-cycles, affix it to the frame just inside the tool box or battery box so that you spot it whenever the cover is removed.

It is a great mistake to neglect these periodic oil changes, for the lubricant in the Honda has a really important job to do. These engines are revving at something like 9,000 r.p.m. If the thin film of lubricant which is interposed between the working surfaces should break down the amount of wear which can occur in a short time is incredible. Moreover, the oil has not just one job to do but several. It lubricates the engine. It also lubricates the gearbox. And it has to help keep the inside of the unit at working temperature, the heat which it absorbs being dissipated through the finned crankcase.

In use, the oil becomes dirty. Condensation inside the unit causes a certain admixture of water (for every gallon of petrol which is burned the engine produces a gallon of water, and not all of this is expelled through the exhaust) and sludge results. By the end of the specified oil-change period the oil is thus contaminated with dirt, water, and tiny metal particles and is no longer capable of doing its job properly. If it is left inside the engine the wear rate is stepped up and efficiency suffers. For this reason, it is vital to adhere to the oil-change periods which are specified by the manufacturers.

For much the same reasons only the recommended grades of oil should be used. These recommendations are the result of long and expensive tests by the factory and by the oil companies. I have seen some of these under way at oil research centres and, believe me, they are thorough. By the time they are over, the technicians know exactly what lubricant will give least friction and longest life in any given engine. So I, for one, gratefully accept their advice and never begrudge the few pence which it costs to keep the engine well supplied with clean fresh oil of the right type.

Oil changes are best carried out at the end of a run, when the oil is hot. The reason for this is pretty obvious. Heat makes oil more viscous—it will run far more easily than when cold. Consequently, removal of the sump drain plug leads to an immediate and strong flow of oil out of the engine, and this carries with it most of the impurities which have collected there during the miles since the previous oil change. One word of warning, though. Always remove the oil filler plug after taking out the drain plug, or there may be a tendency for internal suction to hold back some of the dirty oil.

In all cases Honda drain plugs are located centrally underneath the engine. On the single-cylinder machines the drain plug is the 16 mm

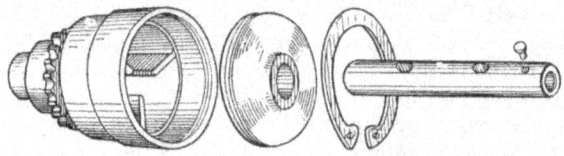

FIG. 22. OIL FILTER ELEMENT, 250/305 c.c. MODELS
This type of centrifugal oil filter is employed on the bigger Honda twins. To clean it, the securing circlip must be released.

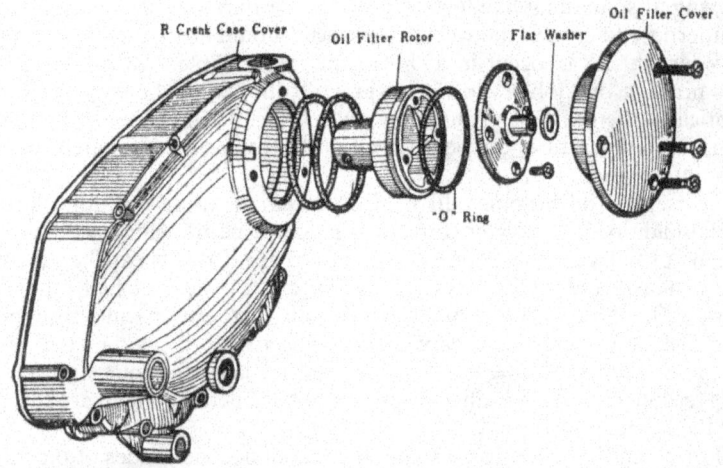

FIG. 23. OIL FILTER ELEMENT, 125 c.c. TWINS
Four countersunk screws hold the end of the oil filter element on the smaller twins. Cleaning is similar to that of the bigger machines.

headed plug found immediately under the curved section of the crankcase casting. Both the 125 c.c. twins have the drain plug positioned centrally. A 17 mm spanner is needed to remove it. On the 250 c.c. and 304 c.c. machines the 17 mm drain plug is at the front end of the finned plate on which the oil pump is mounted.

Frequently, these plugs are very tight and it is essential for a good ring spanner of the correct size to be available. If necessary, the end of the spanner may be tapped with a hammer to help loosen a tight plug.

All twin-cylinder Hondas have centrifugal oil filters, which must be dismantled and cleaned at each oil change. On the 125 c.c. models the filter is located behind a circular plate at the front of the unit, on the right-hand side. On the bigger machines it is behind a similar plate, but on the left-hand side of the motor-cycle. In each case the cover plate is held down by three recess-headed screws. Again, these may be very tight and efforts to free them by use of the appropriate cross-headed screwdriver alone may result merely in badly chewed screw heads. Unless the screws undo easily, the best course is to butt against each screw in turn a short length of steel rod and tap this briskly with a hammer to jar the threads. When the screws are out the cover may be carefully prised away from the case by inserting a screwdriver into the special slots provided. That done, the oil filter may be pulled out.

Oil filters for 125 c.c. machines are dismantled by undoing four recess-headed screws which hold the oil filter cover to the filter body. Though of similar design the 250 and 305 c.c. twins' filter has a cover retained by a large circlip. This can be removed by the use of special circlip pliers or by carefully prising it out of its housing.

Centrifugal oil filters should be well washed in petrol and then allowed to drain thoroughly before being reassembled. When refitting the filter make sure that the rubber O-rings used behind the cover plates are in good condition. If in doubt fit new rings, or oil leakages may develop.

CHAPTER VII

MAINTAINING THE SINGLE-CYLINDER MODELS

To keep the single-cylinder Honda engine running well only a minimum of normal maintenance is required. The tappets, the plug gap, and the contact-breaker gap should be checked as advised and adjustments made when necessary. Finally the oil should be changed at the recommended intervals.

Checking the tappets. It must be stressed that with the Honda engines correct tappet adjustment is vital. Since the clearance is very fine indeed —only 0·002 to 0·004 of an inch—great care has to be exercised in this job. The engine must be completely cold. If it is hot, or even only slightly warm, it will be impossible to make an accurate reading. As a general rule it is better to check the tappets first thing in the morning or when the engine has stood without being run for at least five or six hours.

Wipe the area around the screwed rocker box caps with clean rag, so that there is no possibility of dirt or grit entering the engine. Then remove both caps. Next bring the piston to T.D.C. on the compression stroke. This is found most easily by removing the flywheel cover on the left side of the crankcase and turning the engine over until the mark on the flywheel coincides with the mark scribed on the crankcase. The appropriate feeler gauge is then slipped between the tappets and the inlet and exhaust valves in turn to test the clearance. Though it should slide in easily there should be no perceptible up-and-down play possible. If the feeler is left in position you should not be able to either lift or depress the rocker. Your fingers are very sensitive instruments and can detect even minor amounts of play, so if movement can be felt some degree of adjustment is necessary. A tight tappet is worse than a loose one. If the gauge won't fit adjust at once.

Adjusting the Tappets. Each tappet consists of a short length of screwed rod locked in place on the rocker's adjuster end by a 10 mm lock nut. Before adjustment can be made this nut must be loosened. Don't overdo things though. It is sufficient to undo it only a few turns—just enough to release the adjuster so that the tappet can be moved up and down by revolving the adjuster in the rocker.

Where a tight tappet has been discovered, slacken off the adjuster until the feeler gauge slips easily into the gap. With a loose tappet, insert the gauge and tighten the adjuster. I find it best, incidentally, always to keep

MAINTAINING THE SINGLE-CYLINDER MODELS 51

the spanner on the lock nut throughout this operation so that the setting can be locked down to enable interim checks to be made. Vary the setting of the adjuster until the gauge will just slip into the gap with no up-and-down play on the rocker. Then, keeping the adjuster absolutely still, retighten the lock nut to hold the new setting. That done, check the gap again—for it is remarkably easy to move the adjuster slightly when tightening the lock nut and this results in the setting being deranged. If this has happened loosen the lock nut a thread or so and readjust. When you are satisfied that both tappets are correctly set replace the rocker caps and the magneto cover.

Checking the Sparking Plug Gap. Bearing in mind that sparking plugs work in a combustion chamber at temperatures many times greater than that of an oven, it is hard to believe that it is possible to maintain a gap between two metallic points with any degree of accuracy. In fact it is not only possible but vital. Though the plug will continue to work with a gap which is wildly incorrect it will not permit the engine to give of its best. Hence the importance of regular checks.

To check the plug, detach the pull-off cap carrying the H.T. lead and, using the box spanner provided in the tool kit, unscrew the plug from the head. On a new machine the plug is often a very tight fit, and under these circumstances it is permissible to tap the tommy bar sharply with a hammer to help the initial loosening. Using a feeler gauge measure the gap between the central and the side electrode of the plug. It should be 0·024 of an inch. If there is any significant variation from this, adjustment will be required.

Adjusting the Sparking Plug Gap. Gap adjustment is simple—it merely involves moving the side electrode nearer to or further from the centre electrode. Before doing so clean the plug. The best method is by sand blasting (a garage will carry this job out, and set the gap as specified, for sixpence or so) but in the home workshop a stiff bristled brush usually has to stand in for the job.

Brush the electrodes carefully, making sure that the bristles reach *underneath* the side electrode, and try to ease out any carbon deposits between the inner sides of the body and the nose of the insulator. That done, insert a feeler gauge into the plug gap and check the gap, for brushing away deposits may have altered it. If the gap is too wide leave the feeler in place and very gently tap with a spanner or the handle of a screwdriver on the top edge of the side electrode. This bends it slightly towards the centre electrode. By moving the feeler gauge in and out while you are doing this you will be able to feel exactly when the electrodes begin to bear against the feeler. The gap will then be correct. Where the gap is too small to allow the correct feeler to enter, the side electrode must be moved away from the centre electrode. It can be bent upwards by lifting it with a small screwdriver, or by use of one of the special gap-setting tools sold by accessories shops.

Never attempt to alter a plug gap by bending the centre electrode. This would inevitably fracture the ceramic insulator, and the plug will then have to be discarded. A fractured insulator would normally permit the current to short-circuit itself to earth and so prevent the engine running. On the other hand, the engine might continue to run while the broken section of insulator disintegrated inside. This would result in highly-abrasive particles falling into the engine with disastrous effects on the cylinder bore, the piston, and the rings.

Checking the Contact-breaker Gap: Models C.100, C.110, and C.114. First of all remove the flywheel cover completely. Then rotate the flywheel until the points—which can be seen through the inspection slots in the flywheel face—are fully open. This position has to be found by inspection, and to aid vision here it is sometimes advisable to insert a thin piece of white paper (a cigarette paper is ideal) behind the points.

When the fully-open position has been found, insert a 0·014 in. feeler into the gap and check that it will slide freely, but without up-and-down movement. If so, the gap is correct. Be careful, however, not to be misled by an overtight gap which can be opened up a little by easing the gauge in. This gives a distinctive "notchy" feel as the gauge is inserted, rather akin to that of a key which has been "wangled" into an unlubricated lock.

Model C.102. Remove the points cover, rotate the crankshaft till the points are fully open, and test the gap with a 0·014 in. feeler. As the contacts are fully exposed this is an altogether easier job than with other models in the range, and full visual inspection should be possible.

Adjusting the Contact-breaker Gap: Model C.102. When setting the gap between the contacts the short red line which is stamped on the face of the contact-breaker cam should coincide with the fibre heel on the moving arm of the breaker unit. Set the crankshaft to this position. Then release the two screws which hold the fixed contact plate. Do not undo these fully—merely loosen them sufficiently for the plate to move when the small eccentric adjusting screw is turned. Insert a 0·014 in. feeler gauge and alter the position of the eccentric with a thin-bladed screwdriver until the gauge is a sliding fit in the gap between the points. Then, holding the eccentric completely still, lock up the two fixing screws.

Subsequently reinsert the feeler gauge and check that the setting has not altered while you were tightening the screw. If it has, it will be necessary to carry out the procedure again to obtain exactly the right gap.

Models C.100, C.110, and C.114. It must be realized that on these models there is no provision for altering the timing of the spark by turning the stator plate and timing adjustment is therefore made by increasing or decreasing the contact-breaker points gap.

To set the gap, turn the flywheel until the points are fully open and then measure the gap with feeler gauges. It should be 0·014 in. If adjustment is needed loosen the large cheese-headed screw which secures the contact-breaker base plate and insert a screwdriver into the slot in the rear edge of the plate. Twisting the screwdriver will move the plate and so increase or decrease the gap. When the correct gap has been obtained lock the screw—and then recheck the gap. If it has altered during the locking up, loosen the screw again and readjust.

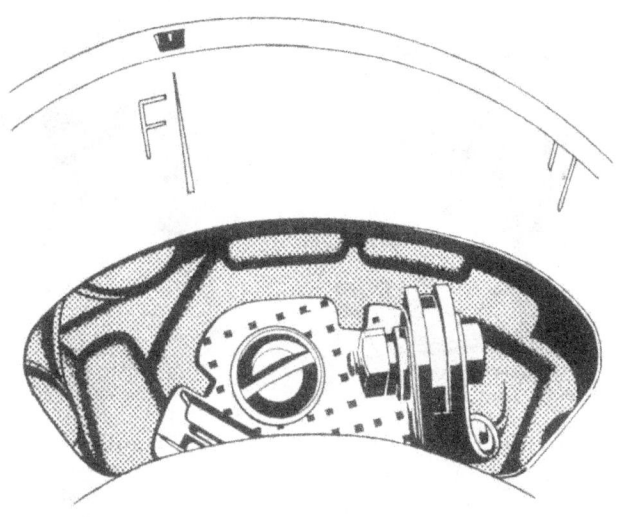

Fig. 24. Contact Points and Timing, Model C.100

With the "F" mark on the flywheel aligned with the line on the crankcase, the contact points should just be opening. This is the only timing adjustment possible on the Models C.100, C.110, and C.114 Hondas.

Checking the Timing: Models C.100, C.110, and C.114. After setting the gap turn the flywheel *anti-clockwise* until the mark "F" on the flywheel coincides with the indented line on the flywheel casing. The points should now be just beginning to open—which means that a 1½ thou (0·0015 in.) feeler gauge can just be slipped between them. If it cannot it means that the points are still closed and the ignition timing is retarded—that is, the spark will be occurring too late. If the points are opening before the two marks coincide the ignition is over-advanced and the spark is too early.

In either case the points gap will need resetting. If ignition is retarded the gap must be increased slightly; if it is advanced then the gap must be reduced. After each adjustment, which is made with the points fully open as described above, turn the flywheel anti-clockwise to the two marks for a timing check. This is essential, for upon the correct timing depends much of the efficiency of the engine.

Clutch Adjustment: Models C.100 and C.102. With its three-way coupling, the fully-automatic Honda clutch is in itself a miniature masterpiece of engineering. It is brought into operation, first, by the effect of engine speed. As crankshaft revolutions increase, eight hardened steel rollers are subjected to centrifugal force and move outwards along tapered

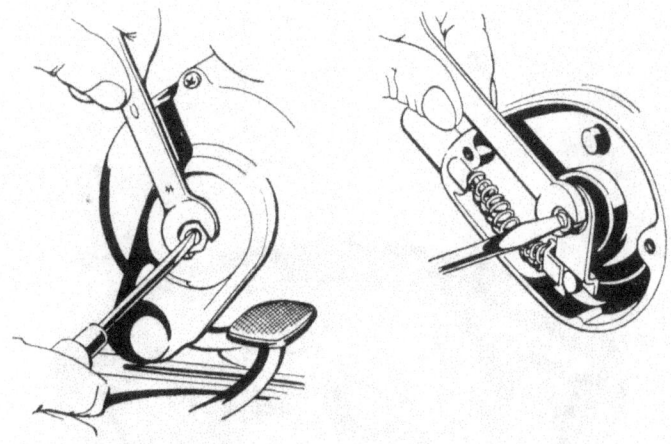

FIG. 25. CLUTCH ADJUSTMENT ON SINGLES

On the Models C.100 and C.102 (*left, above*) the clutch is adjusted by means of this external screw and lock nut. On the C.110 and C.114 machines, the adjusting screw and lock nut are beneath an alloy cover (*right, above*) and there is also an adjuster on the clutch cable.

tracks. Their movement is utilized to increase the pressure on the clutch plates and so take up the drive. In addition the clutch can be brought into operation by the action of the rear wheel over-running the engine when a gear is engaged—as, for example, in push starting. This same mechanism makes kick starting possible. It comprises a quick-acting three-start thread incorporated in an extension of the drive gear. Lastly, there is a direct connexion between the gear-change spindle and the clutch-withdrawal mechanism, so that the clutch is operated whenever the gear-change pedal is used.

Adjustment of the clutch is infrequently required. Unless there are unmistakable signs of clutch slip or of drag, therefore, this component should be left untouched. However, when adjustment becomes necessary it is extremely simple to carry out. In the centre of the clutch housing on the right side of the engine will be found a screw and lock nut. Slacken the nut and turn the screw clockwise to move the clutch-operating cam plate away from the release mechanism. Full spring and roller pressures then operate on the clutch. Now turn the screw anti-clockwise until pressure can be felt on it. Stop turning immediately, and slacken the screw by a quarter of a turn in the clockwise direction. Still holding the screw, retighten the lock nut.

Models C.110 and C.114. Unlike the scooterettes, the small Honda motor-cycles have a manually-operated clutch mechanism whose adjustment is extremely sensitive.

To reach the adjuster on the clutch-operating arm the pear-shaped cover on the right side of the crankcase must first be removed. This is held by two recess-headed screws. Now check that there is roughly a quarter of an inch of free play in the clutch control cable, and if not rack the cable adjuster in or out until this is obtained. You can then proceed with adjustment of the arm.

First slacken off the 10 mm lock nut on the centre adjuster screw and then rotate the screw anti-clockwise with a screwdriver by about an eighth or quarter of a turn. This ensures that there is no contact between the screw and the push rod which operates the clutch. Next rotate the screw clockwise until pressure is felt. Immediately, turn it back again in an anti-clockwise direction for just one eighth of a turn. Hold the screw steady with the screwdriver and tighten the lock nut to hold the new setting. Now make a fresh check on the control cable's free play. There must be just an eighth of an inch—no more and certainly no less. Use the cable adjuster on the crankcase to obtain this play. Finally, check that the clutch is freeing properly by kicking the engine over with the clutch disengaged. That done, release the clutch and kick the engine again to make sure that there is no slip.

Honda stress that when adjusting clutches on these models it is vital that the adjusting screw should *never* be screwed inwards against the pressure of the clutch springs. If this is done the plate which locates the three hardened balls will drop out of place. Should this happen, the entire clutch cover has to come off before they can be refitted.

Carburettor Fuel Tap: Models C.100 and C.102. Both scooterettes are fitted with Keihin DP.13 HOV. carburettors of identical design—downdraught units in which the float chamber is held to the mixing chamber by a pair of countersunk screws, with the fuel tap incorporated into the float chamber top.

Very little trouble is ever encountered with these carburettors, but some cases of fuel starvation due to a faulty tap washer have been reported. If this is suspected, first obtain the necessary replacement washer (Part No. DP.13/137) and then drain the fuel tank. This can be done by syphoning out the fuel with a length of plastic hose, or simply by removing the fuel line at the carburettor end and allowing the petrol to drain into a can.

Remove the front shielding. This is held by two bolts and a clamping nut on each side of the machine, and also by the air filter cover. This must be taken off before pulling the shield clear. To dismantle the tap remove the two screws which secure the tap cover and lift the cover, the spring washer, and the tap lever. Under the lever is the packing washer. Take out the old washer and discard it. Check that the fuel passages are clear and, if so, fit the new washer and reassemble the tap.

Carburettor Needle Adjustment: Models C.100 and C.102. Generally speaking, little in the way of adjustment is either necessary or desirable on Honda machines, and it is possible to do more harm than good by inexpert tuning. For this reason, it is essential to note carefully by how much any adjustment is altered from the original factory setting. Then, if an experiment is carried out, it is always possible to restore the correct setting.

Misfiring at intermediate speeds is an occasional complaint, and quite often it proves to be due to an over-rich mixture. The composition of the mixture in the intermediate range of engine speeds (from 4,500 to 8,500 r.p.m. approx.) is controlled by a combination of throttle slide cutaway and the needle jet setting. Though the cutaway cannot be adjusted, the needle can.

To reach the needle screw off the top of the mixing chamber—the part where the control cable enters the instrument—and carefully withdraw the chamber top complete with return spring, slide, and needle. Detach the slide and needle by holding the chamber top and the cable, and pressing the slide upwards against the resistance of the spring. As the nipple on the end of the cable clears its seating in the slide, edge it to the outside and gently slide it through its slot. The needle/slide assembly is now clear.

A W-shaped needle clip plate holds the needle and clip in the slide. Ease this plate out by pressing the needle upwards *with your fingers*. Do not try pressing the needle on any other surface or there will be a risk of distortion. When the needle has been removed note in which slot the clip has been placed. Standard settings are in either the third or fourth notch from the top. Ease the clip off the needle and replace it *one notch* nearer the top. This has the effect of seating the needle lower in the slide, and consequently weakens the mixture slightly in the intermediate ranges.

Replace the clip and needle in the slide, and spring in the clip plate. Offer up the slide assembly to the cable. You will find it possible to compress the spring and work the cable through its slot, finally easing the nipple back into the seating. Wipe the slide clean with non-fluffy rag, and reinsert it in the mixing chamber. Remember that it is located by a peg, which engages in a slot in the slide and prevents it from turning. If the slide will not enter easily *don't* force it—it means that the peg is not engaging. Twisting the slide gently from side to side will allow the peg to take up in its slot. The whole assembly is then pushed home and the chamber top screwed down.

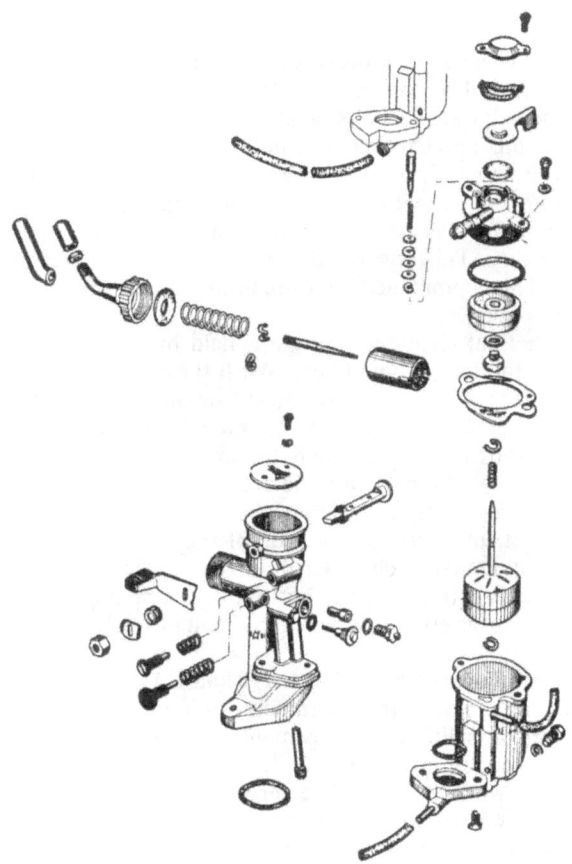

FIG. 26. KEIHIN CARBURETTOR, C.100 AND C.102

Bolted direct to the cylinder head, this downdraught carburettor has a butterfly-type choke and the fuel tap is in the float chamber top.

Carburettor Tickover Adjustments: Models C.100 and C.102. Tickover is regulated by two screws on the carburettor body. They are the throttle stop screw, which alters the position of the throttle slide relative to the mixing chamber, and the air adjusting screw. The throttle stop is mounted centrally on the side of the body and the air screw higher and to the right.

The correct setting of the air screw is 1–1¼ turns out. With the screw so set the tickover speed is regulated simply by racking the throttle stop screw in or out until a reliable tickover is obtained. It is best to do this with the engine hot and after checking that no air leaks exist at the flange joint.

Carburettor Cleaning: Models C.100 and C.102. Remove the front shielding, as described earlier, and detach the air cleaner hose and the fuel pipe. Detach the two bolts holding the carburettor to its flange after removing the mixing chamber top, pulling out the slide, and taping the entire throttle assembly to the frame tube to protect it from damage. The carburettor can now be lifted from the engine.

Before stripping, wash it thoroughly in a bowl of clean petrol and dry it with clean rag. This ensures that no dirt will inadvertently enter the instrument. Then commence the dismantling process, working on sheets of clean newspaper.

Remove the float chamber top cover, held by two screws, and lift off the cover and the screen-type filter. Wash these in clean petrol. Detach the float chamber, which is secured to the mixing chamber by two screws beneath its flange, and screw out the main jet from its housing in the flange. Clean it by blowing through it from the top end, and then replace it. Detach each of the remaining jets one by one, treating them in the same way, and replacing each before the next is removed. They are the slow-running jet, mounted on the side of the carburettor just off-centre of the horizontal mixing chamber, and the needle jet which is located under a plug concentric with the bottom of the mixing chamber. When rebuilding the carburettor, use new gaskets and washers throughout.

Carburettor Adjustment: Models C.110 and C.114. Apart from the fact that the fuel tap is not in the instrument itself and that the actual layout of the carburettor is different, adjustment of the Keihin PW.16 instrument fitted to these models should be carried out as described in the sections relating to the Model C.100. The throttle screw, which has a knurled head, is set immediately above the pivot point for the float chamber clip and the air adjuster screw is set at an angle to its left.

Carburettor Cleaning: Models C.110 and C.114. Detach the mixing chamber top and draw out the throttle slide assembly. Tape the assembly out of harm's way. Detach the oil feed unions (which carry warm oil to the choke area), the fuel pipe, and unbolt the carburettor from the frame. Slide the instrument off its rubber hose and wash it in clean petrol. Then dry it with non-fluffy rag. Spread out clean newspaper to work on, and have a small bowl of petrol at hand for washing purposes.

Prise off the spring clip holding the float chamber to the body. Take out the hinge pin on which the twin floats pivot, and place them on one side. The needle valve can then be removed for cleaning. Projecting down from the body is the hexagonal needle jet holder with the main jet in its base. Remove both for cleaning. When the holder is out the needle

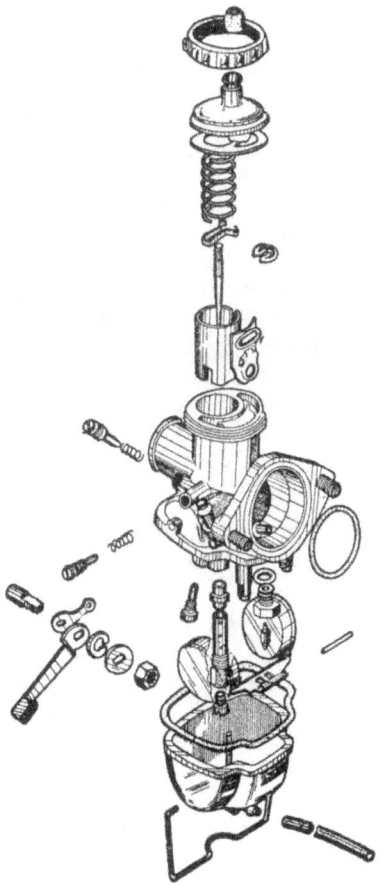

FIG. 27. KEIHIN CARBURETTOR, C.110 AND C.114

On this carburettor the choke is of slide type and an unusual feature is that hot oil is circulated past the mixing chamber to prevent icing.

jet itself can be carefully pushed downwards and out of the carburettor body. Clean each jet by blowing through it from the far end and wash it in petrol. Then replace them and take out the pilot jet which will be found just to the side of the main jet. Clean this and then replace it. Wash the floats and float chamber. Examine the floats for any signs of damage. To test for leakage, shake the float assembly. If petrol has entered you will hear it swill around inside.

Rebuild the carburettor using new gaskets throughout. Make sure that the float needle is fitted properly, with the taper end bearing on the valve seating. To test for the correct petrol level invert the carburettor with the float chamber bowl removed. The float needle spring will then be depressed by the weight of the floats. Carefully tilt the carburettor until it is between fifty and seventy degrees out of the vertical and measure the distance between the carburettor body base and the outer periphery of the float. It should be exactly 19·5 mm, though it suffices if the distance lies between 19 mm and 20 mm. To alter the petrol level bend the float tongue very gently, and recheck the measurement. But be particularly careful not to alter the position of the individual floats in doing so.

Air Cleaners: All Models. Paper-type air filters are used on all 50 c.c. Hondas. On the C.100 and C.102 the filter is mounted on the frame tube just behind the steering head, and on the small motor-cycles it is on the right side of the machine beneath a plastic cover.

In the first case, unscrewing one domed nut and lifting an alloy cover bares the filter, and removal of a second nut enables it to be lifted out. In the motor-cycles, remove the cover by undoing the knurled screw and then take the filter from its place.

Clean the filter by dusting it with a soft brush. You can also use a tyre pump to blow away surface dirt. Make sure that the element is not damaged or fouled by oil, then refit it.

Cleaning Fuel Tap: Models C.110 and C.114. The filter bowl is screwed to the bottom of the fuel tap and can be removed by use of a 10 mm ring spanner or socket. Do *not* use an open-ended spanner. It may also be necessary to support the tap with an appropriate-sized spanner while undoing the bowl. Lift out the synthetic rubber sealing washer and the filter screen. Wash the screen and the bowl in petrol, and then refit them.

Brake Adjustment: All Models. Screw-type adjusters are provided for all brakes. Take up wear by turning the adjusters half a turn at a time. They have a "click" action. Continue adjustment until the brake is felt to bind when the wheel is turned. Then slacken off, half a turn at a time, until binding disappears. Check the efficiency of the brakes regularly.

Wheel Removal: All Models. To detach the front wheel place a suitable wooden block under the crankcase so that the wheel is clear of the ground. Disconnect the brake adjuster nut and take out the nut and bolt which, on the C.110 and C.114 variants, secures the brake plate to the anchorage arm. Disconnect the speedometer at the drive end, take out the front axle split pin, and undo the spindle nut. The axle can now be pulled out of the hollow wheel spindle, and the wheel will be displaced from the two fork links. Finally free it by removing the brake cable from its housing on the backplate.

To take out the rear wheel disconnect the rear brake rod adjusting nut

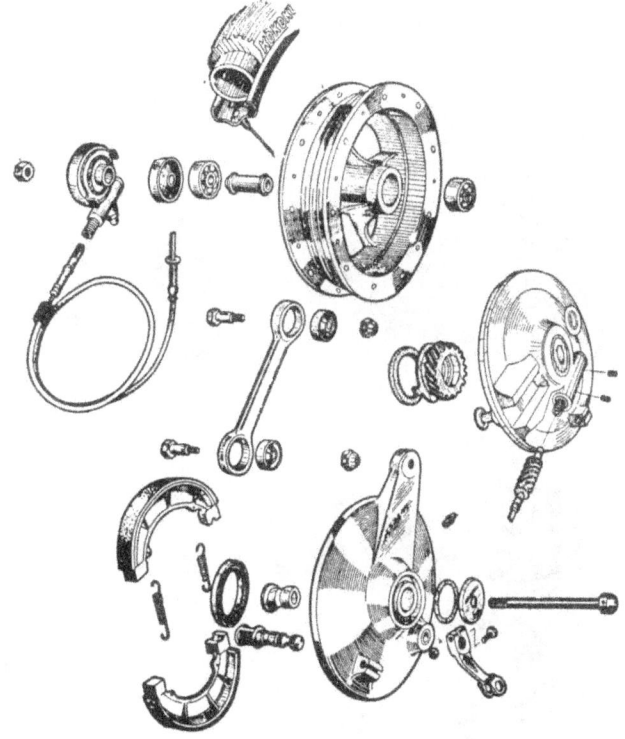

FIG. 28. FRONT BRAKE AND HUB, C.100 AND C.102

On early versions of the Honda a backplate secured by a torque arm was used. Later models have the slotted type of backplate. Otherwise the front brakes of all models are of similar design. Both types are shown here.

and take off the nut and spring clip securing the brake anchor arm. Remove the 17 mm nut on the rear axle and pull the axle out. The tubular distance piece on the right side between the brake and the fork can now be lifted away and the wheel is simply pulled to the right to free it from the drive and then dropped out.

Silencer: Models C.110 and C.114. Cleaning the baffle tube of the silencer is recommended every 2,500 miles. To reach it, detach the 5 mm screw which is to be found at the end of the silencer and draw out the

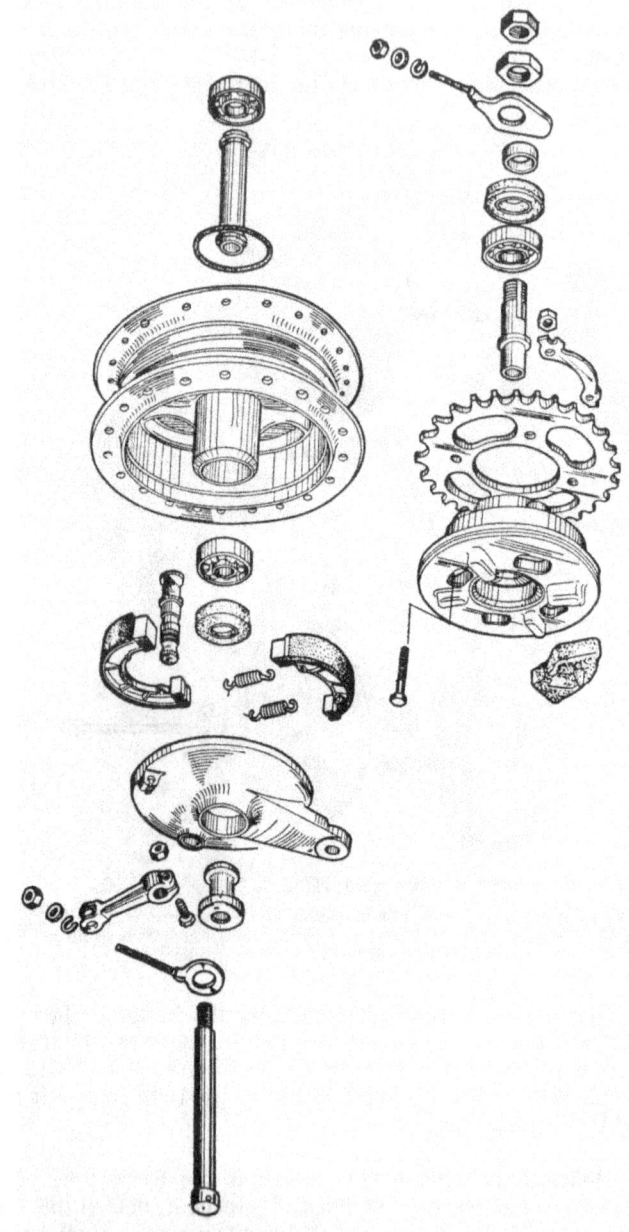

Fig. 29. Rear Brake and Hub, C.100 and C.102

Quickly detachable, the rear wheel also incorporates a shock absorber in which rubber blocks (only one is shown here) are placed between vanes on the hub and drive member. It smooths the power delivery.

MAINTAINING THE SINGLE-CYLINDER MODELS

baffle tube. Unblock all holes and brush away all carbon deposits. If this is neglected, performance may be adversely affected.

Bulbs: All Models. To reach the headlamp, speedometer, and neutral-indicator bulbs remove the front of the headlamp, which is held by a recess-headed screw. To reach indicator and rear lamp bulbs take off the appropriate lens assembly by removing the recess-headed screws which secure them.

Stoplight Timing. The stoplight switch in each case is operated from the brake pedal through the medium of a spring. If the light is lighting too late—or is not lighting at all—it indicates that greater tension is required. Loosen the lower switch lock nut and lift the switch by screwing the top nut downwards. This advances the operation of the stoplight. When the light is coming on at the desired amount of pedal movement retighten the lower nut. To make it light later, reverse this procedure.

Chain Adjustment: All Models. Driving chains are adjusted by pulling the rear wheel backwards by means of drawbolts. To do so loosen the rear axle nut, and then the nuts on the drawbolts should be turned one flat at a time to tension the chain. After each nut has been moved by this amount check the up-and-down play on the lower chain run through the hole in the chain case, normally closed by a push-in plug. Total movement must not be less than 0·4 nor more than 0·8 of an inch. When the correct play has been achieved, retighten the axle nut. Finally check that the guide marks on the left and right drawbolts are in the same relative positions. There are corresponding marks on the fork members. If the marks on both sides do not coincide the drawbolt setting must be altered so that the wheel comes into correct alignment. Naturally, the chain tension will then have to be rechecked. Always test tension with the machine off the stand and with a rider aboard.

Battery: All Models. Batteries require little care—but they demand it regularly. The battery loses part of the water component in its acid when it is in use. This loss must be made good by adding *distilled water* to bring the electrolyte level back to the upper level mark on the battery casing. This water is added by detaching the battery from the machine —it is held by a clamp which has a single locking bolt, and by its two leads which are bolted to it. Then take out the cell plugs and, using a suction-type filler, add the distilled water to each cell in turn. Clean the terminal posts and lead terminals with emery cloth, rubbing each until the metal is bright, and coat them with Vaseline before refitting the battery.

CHAPTER VIII

TOP OVERHAULS, SINGLES

As one of the main objects of home maintenance is to save money, there is very little point in attempting to strip one of the 50 c.c. Honda power units completely. These engines are engineered, of necessity, to extremely fine limits. Therefore, an extensive kit of special tools is needed for work of this nature. Since such a kit can cost upwards of £20 its acquisition is not economic, and it is better to entrust the very rare complete overhaul to an agent's well-equipped workshop. However, for the benefit of enthusiasts who wish to know what is involved I have set out the basic stripping procedure at the end of this chapter.

Most of us, I think, are more likely to wish to save the odd pound on top overhauls—a job which is well within the average owner's compass. This can be done with the engine still mounted in the frame, too, which is a distinct advantage for those who lack workshop facilities.

Detach the front shielding by releasing its four securing bolts, two clamping screws, and the single centre nut holding the air filter cover. Lift the shield from the machine. Then, using a paintbrush, coat the entire engine unit with grease solvent. Work this into the cylinder fins, and into all the odd corners. Next, wash the solvent away with water trickled on from a garden hose, and then give the engine time to dry off. I normally let mine stand overnight.

Stripping. C.100 and C.102

When the components are dry stripping can begin—but before you do this make certain you have all the tools, materials, and spares which you need. They are a decoke set comprising new gaskets for the rocker cover and cylinder head joint, new rubber oil seals for the oil drain and pushrod tunnels, a copper/asbestos ring for the exhaust port, and new valve springs. Fine grinding paste is another necessity, together with some clean petrol and a suitable bowl so that components can be washed. For clearing carbon a scraper will be wanted, and for removing the valves a small valve-spring compressor.

As a first step take off the auxiliaries—the carburettor, the dirt shield, and the exhaust pipe. Detach the plug cap and take out the plug. All this is straightforward. The carburettor merely demands removal of the mixing chamber top and slide and the fuel pipe. But remember that the tank must be drained, or some suitable plug made up ready to prevent the fuel from flowing out of the pipe since the tap is on the carburettor. Take off the air hose. Only two 10 mm nuts then hold the carburettor to the barrel.

The dirt shield is held by four 10 mm nuts and the exhaust pipe by two 10 mm nuts at the cylinder head and two 10 mm set screws at the silencer support bracket.

Stripping. C.110 and C.114

Follow the above sequence, with the exception of the carburettor and dirt shield. For the carburettor, follow the instructions in the previous chapter.

Head Removal. Now take off the rocker feed oil pipe, using a 10 mm spanner on its two banjo unions, and the two rocker cover inspection

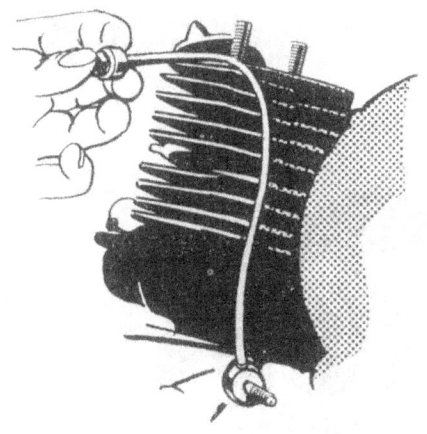

FIG. 30. HEAD REMOVAL, SINGLES, STAGE ONE

First, the exhaust pipe, the carburettor, dirt shield, etc. having been removed, the oil feed pipe to the rocker box is detached at both ends.

caps, each of which has a 17 mm hexagon. Take off the four 10 mm bolts which hold the rocker box and lift this away from the cylinder head. Spin the pushrods round to free them, and then pull them out.

A further four nuts hold the actual cylinder head. Remove all the nuts, and slide the head off its studs. If the joint is difficult to break, cover the head with a pad of cloth and jar it with the heel of your hand. *Never* try to insert a screwdriver into the head joint or the head and barrel may be irreparably damaged.

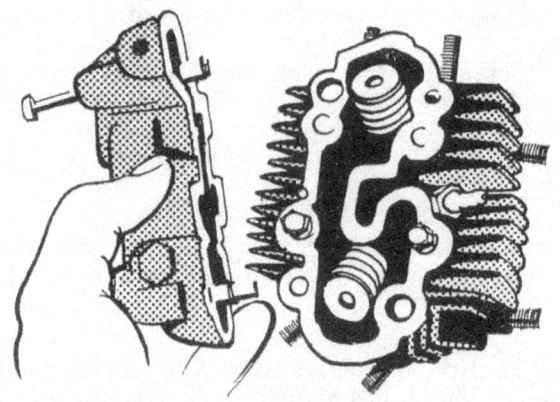

Fig. 31. Head Removal, Singles, Stage Two

Next the bolts securing the rocker box to the head are undone. Then lift off the box and withdraw the two pushrods from their tunnels.

Fig. 32. Head Removal, Singles, Stage Three

Now the four head nuts are taken off and the head is free to come off its studs. Should it stick, jar it with the heel of your hand.

Barrel Removal. Once the head has been taken off, removing the barrel is merely a matter of sliding the cylinder off its studs. Support the piston as it emerges from the lower end of the cylinder, or it may fall against the engine and be damaged.

FIG. 33. BARREL REMOVAL, SINGLES

With the head off the barrel can slide from the studs. Support the piston as it leaves the bore, to prevent it being damaged.

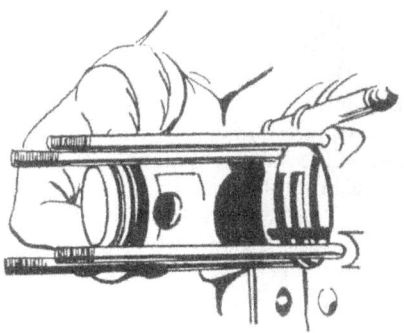

FIG. 34. PISTON REMOVAL, SINGLES

Detach the circlips at each end of the gudgeon pin. Warm the piston with rag well wrung out in hot water. This expands the light alloy. The gudgeon pin can then be pressed out of the piston bosses easily.

Piston Removal. Two circlips position the gudgeon pin in the piston boss. Use circlip pliers to release these and then gently tap the pin out of the boss. If it is hard to move soak rags in hot water, wring them out, then wrap them round the piston and leave them for a minute or two. This will expand the metal slightly and make the pin easier to move.

Valve Removal. Slide the valve-removing tool over the valve head, with its feet on the valve cap. Screw the tool down until the springs have been compressed enough to free the collets which secure the valve stem in the cap. Remove the collets and release the tool. The valve, spring, and cap can then be lifted out. Mark the head of each valve to identify it.

Carbon Removal. With the scraper, clear all carbon away from the inside of the cylinder head and from the exhaust port interior. Make sure that the area around the plug hole is clear. Finish off by using wire wool to give a good surface finish.

Similarly clean both valves, including that section of each valve stem which is exposed inside the ports. Do not scrape or polish the area which is already bright. This is the working surface inside the valve guide.

Gently lift out the piston rings by expanding them slightly with the thumbs. Scrape the piston crown clear of carbon, and finish off with wire wool. You may, if you wish, polish both the inside of the combustion chamber and the piston crown with metal polish, but do *not* use emery cloth. Check that the ring grooves are clear of carbon, and that there is no carbon behind the rings themselves. If there is, use a piece of broken ring as a groove scraper and a blunt penknife to clean the rings. Under no circumstances must the outer surfaces of the rings be touched.

Valve Seating. Honda advise refacing any valve on which pit marks do not exceed a depth of 0·006/0·007 of an inch. Any which have deeper pitting than this should be renewed completely. You will need to get a Honda agent to face the valves, on a machine, to an angle of forty-five degrees. Pitted seats in the head should be similarly recut.

Before fitting both valves should be lightly ground with a fine grade of paste. Smear the valve face with a thin layer of paste and drop the valve into position. With a broad-bladed screwdriver inserted into the slot in the valve head work the valve from side to side through an arc of about ninety degrees, quickly, about half a dozen times. Then lift the valve, give it a quarter turn, and repeat the process. Carry on with this sequence until both valve and seat have a thin but continuous grey line around them. The grinding is then complete.

At this stage, remove the valves and *wash them and the head thoroughly in clean petrol*. Every trace of the abrasive grinding paste must be removed before assembly or it may enter the engine and cause very serious wear. Also wash the piston if metal polish is used on the crown.

Reassembly. Rebuilding the engine is virtually a simple reversal of the stripping procedure, but there are one or two points to watch. You will find that the piston rings are marked with the word "Top" and obviously this mark must be uppermost. The top ring is a chrome type and the lower ring a slotted scraper design. Fit this from the skirt end of the piston.

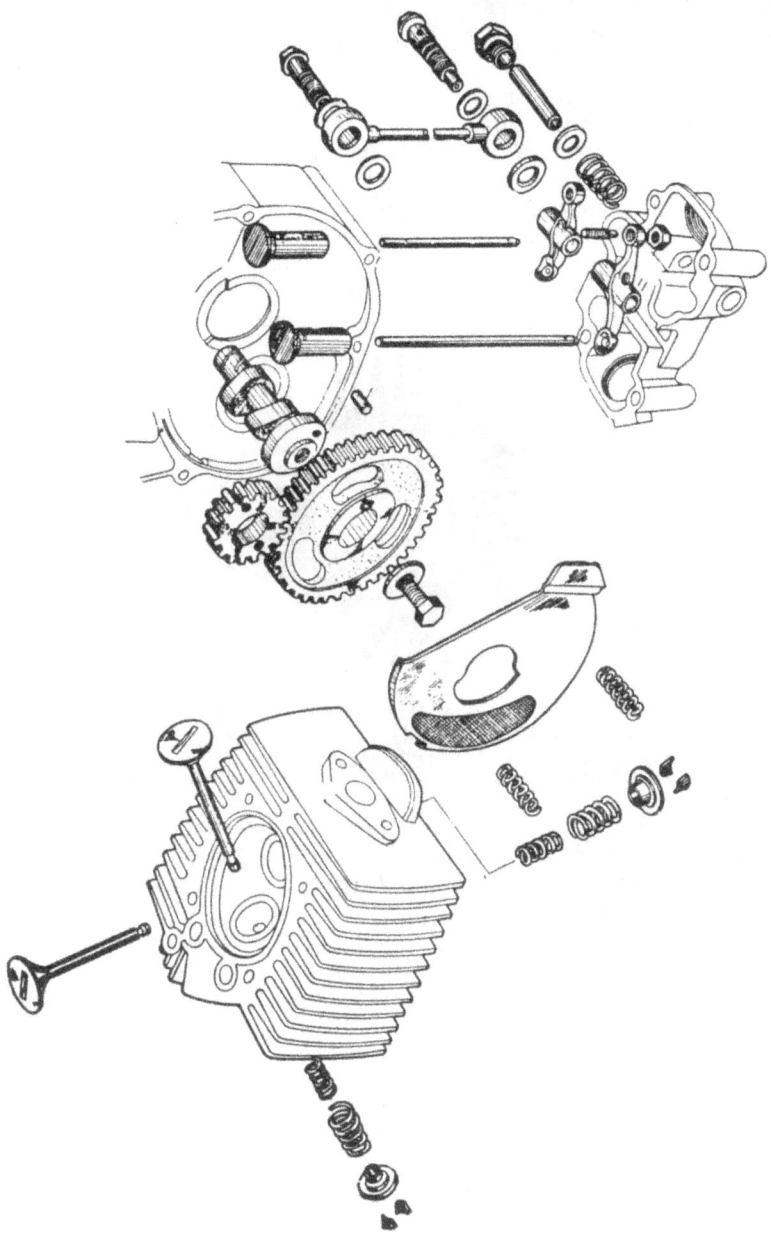

FIG. 35. VALVE GEAR, SINGLES

This exploded view shows clearly the layout of the valve gear. For decarbonizing the valves must be removed from the head and their seats must also be checked for signs of pitting or burning.

Gently ease the middle ring into the centre groove by working from the top, and finally add the top ring.

If the existing piston rings have been reused there will be no need to check the gaps. Where new ones are being fitted, however, they should first be inserted into the bore by themselves, squared up by sliding in the piston from the other end, and the gap between the ring ends measured with a feeler gauge. It should be between 0·003 and 0·010 of an inch, with a maximum permissible gap of 0·039 of an inch. Ring gaps can be widened by gentle use of a very fine file on the ends.

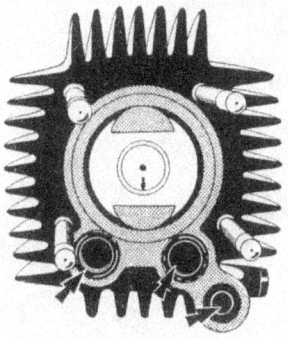

FIG. 36. PISTON FITTING, SINGLES

When refitting the piston to the connecting rod remember that the arrow stamped on its crown must point downwards. After fitting the piston replace the barrel. Do not omit the rubber sealing rings (arrowed) on the pushrod tunnels and oilway.

When refitting the piston be certain that it is the right way round. An arrow is stamped on the crown, and this should point downwards. Lightly oil the bore and slide the barrel on. Compress each ring in turn so that it slips easily into the bore.

Check the length of the old valve springs against the figures given in the appendix. Permissible shortening of the outer springs is 1·4 mm on C.100 and C.102 models, or 0·6 mm on C.110 and C.114 machines. With inner springs shortenings of 1·3 mm and 0·9 mm respectively are permissible, both figures being on free length. If the old springs have passed these limits, use a new set. Employ the valve compressor tool to refit each valve in turn. Bear in mind that the inlet valve is slightly longer than the exhaust valve. Don't mix them up.

Refit the head, using a new gasket, and tighten the head nuts finger-tight at first. Then, using a socket spanner, work from nut to nut, diagonally, taking each up a few threads at a time until the head is securely seated.

Insert the pushrods—the exhaust pushrod is shorter than the inlet one —and replace the rocker cover. Use a new gasket, lightly oiled. Tighten the rocker bolts and reset the tappet clearances. Then complete the assembly work, before attempting to test the engine.

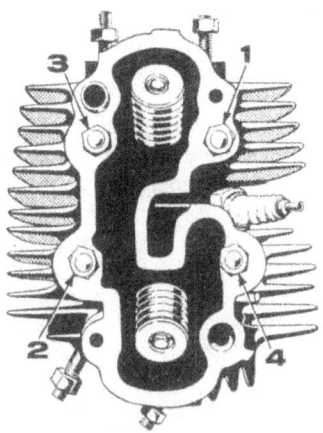

FIG. 37. CYLINDER HEAD NUT TIGHTENING

It is essential that the head should be drawn down evenly by tightening the nuts gradually, working from one to another in the order shown here. If a torque wrench is available, use it. The correct figure is 70 in./lb.

Complete Dismantling. This abridged section is intended simply for the guidance of owners with workshop experience and the requisite set of Honda service tools. I do not advise the average owner to attempt work of this nature.

First remove the engine from the frame by disconnecting the fuel lead, the electrical wiring at the snap connector points, the control cables (to the throttle in the case of the scooterettes, to throttle and clutch on C.110 and C.114 models), and the chain. This latter entails removal of the lower chain case half, the short chain case top cover, and the side cover of the engine on the drive side. The oil must be drained and the battery leads removed.

Detach the carburettor, the footrest assembly, the starter motor feed cables on C.102 models, and unhook the brake and stop-lamp switch springs. Remove the exhaust system. Place a block under the engine unit, take out the upper and lower mounting bolts and lift the engine unit from the frame. On C.110 and C.114 machines the gearchange pedal also has to come off before removing the engine.

Once the unit has been cleaned and is on the bench use the special holding and withdrawal tools to remove the flywheel or, in the case of the C.102, the rotor, and then the stator plate. Lock the final drive sprocket, and remove the two bolts which hold it. Take out the neutral indicator switch, which is held in place by a single recess-headed screw.

Follow the sequence outlined earlier in this chapter for stripping off the head, barrel, and piston.

Nine screws hold the primary drive side cover, removal of which gives access to the clutch. As there is a pair of small compression springs inside the cover—their job is to retain the oil plate in front of the camshaft drive gear—the cover will tend to spring off. Take off the plate, and the anti-rattle spring fitted between the clutch operating cam plate and the release mechanism. Remove the clutch operating lever and washer (from the splined shaft) and the clutch operating cam plate can be lifted away. Then prise the journal ball bearing and carrier from the centre of the clutch drum.

On the C.110 and C.114 the actual clutch dismantling is similar, but the operating pushrod has a lubrication reservoir. An arm is attached to this trough at one end and to the centre of the primary gears shaft at the other. Remove this, and the ball journal and carrier.

Clutch Removal. With the clutch body securely held, free the centre nut's tab washer and release the nut. Slide the clutch off its shaft. To dismantle the clutch unit of C.100 and C.102 models take out the bronze bush from the drive gear centre and, with the drive gear facing upwards, prise out the 101 mm diameter spring ring which is set in a groove in the rear of the clutch body. The drive gear assembly and clutch plates can then be lifted out. There are four small compression springs, on guide pins, whose job is to help free the clutch plates. On the lower plate are guide pins and eight hardened steel rollers. To free the drive plate, the four main springs and the four damper springs release the four cross-headed screws on the front face of the clutch body, loosening each a little at a time. For freeing the clutch drive gear from the clutch centre only removal of the retaining circlip is needed.

On C.110 and C.114 models Honda advise use of a clutch spring compressing tool. First remove the bronze bush from the centre drive gear. Then, with a small screwdriver, prise out the four damper springs which are found in the front face of the clutch housing. With the compressing tool put sufficient pressure on the assembly to free the 101 mm circlip. On releasing the pressure the clutch plates can be lifted out, together with the drive gear and the eight clutch springs.

Camshaft Removal: All Models. Remove the 17 mm circlip from the primary shaft of the gearbox and draw off the driver gear. Take the 23 mm circlip and washer from the kickstarter shaft and disconnect and remove the starter spring. A pair of pointed-nose pliers is needed here. The camshaft can now be taken off, followed by the cam followers. To remove the camshaft timing pinion from the crankshaft a special puller must be used.

Splitting the Crankcase. Once work has reached this stage, the crankcase can be split by removing the nine crankcase bolts and gently tapping around the joint. Also tap the end of the primary gear shaft, the kick-starter shaft, and the crankshaft. When the cases separate the complete gear, kickstarter assembly, and crankshaft will remain in the left case.

Retiming the Valves. To time the valves on reassembly, drive the timing pinion on to the mainshaft using the special tool and mesh the crankshaft pinion tooth marked with a dot into the correspondingly-marked sector of the camshaft wheel.

Fig. 38. Retiming Singles

To obtain the correct valve timing after stripping an engine right down the two marks shown here must be aligned.

CHAPTER IX

WORKING ON THE TWINS

By their very nature the twin-cylinder Hondas are machines which are likely to be owned by out-and-out enthusiasts. Such riders, obviously, do not need to be told how to carry out the few simple jobs which are necessary to keep the Benley and Dream models in good running order. And the suggested check sequence is fully dealt with in Chapter IV.

Perhaps the job most likely to need elucidation is decarbonizing, for contrary to normal practice it is essential to remove the engine completely from the frame before any dismantling of the top half can be carried out. This applies both to 125 and 250 c.c. machines. How this is best done is explained in the stripping sequences which follow.

Engine Removal: Models C.92 and CB.92

1. Remove the footrests. On the C.92 these are formed from a single cross-bar which is bolted at four points to the underside of the crankcase. Footrests on CB.92 models are individual units mounted on plates bolted to either side of the machine. Before the CB.92's left footrest can be detached the gear-change linkage must be released.

2. Detach the exhaust systems. Take off the complete pipe/silencer assembly on each side as one unit.

3. Detach the carburettor covers and the tool box cover.

4. Unbolt the tool tray base and pull out the air cleaner element which is fitted to the inside of the circular cover. Release the element from the carburettor hose by slipping the left hand inside the frame, through the carburettor aperture, and unhooking the hose clip.

5. Release the nut which secures the wiring junction box and then free the clamp. Undo the various snap connectors.

6. Take off the rear section of the left engine cover to gain access to the chain. Disconnect the chain link to break the chain. Then detach the inner section of the cover as well.

7. Release the clutch cable from the control arm.

8. Detach the carburettor.

9. Take off the battery cover, unscrew the clamp bolt and the two terminal bolts, and remove the battery.

10. Release the starter solenoid switch from the frame and disconnect the starter motor cable.

11. Take off the kick starter.

12. Remove the sparking plug caps from the HT leads and ease the leads out of their channels in the cylinder head.

13. Make up a suitable engine support from wood blocks or a stout box and insert it under the crankcase.

14. Take off the nuts from all engine mounting bolts. These are in order: No. 1 bolt in front of and above the rear fork pivot, No. 2 bolt in the upper mounting atop the head, and No. 3 bolt in front of and below the rear fork pivot. Nos. 1 and 3 occur on both sides of the frame.

15. Detach both No. 1 bolts and then both No. 3 bolts.

16. Detach No. 2 bolt. The engine is now free to be lifted on to the bench.

Engine Removal: Models C.72 and C.77

1. Remove the left exhaust system.
2. Detach the left footrest and gear pedal.
3. Take off the left carburettor shield and pull off the vent tube from the head.
4. Detach the left plug cap, the carburettor flange nut, and the breather pipe.
5. Undo the left upper rear engine mounting bolt, located in front of and above the rear fork pivot.
6. Detach the right exhaust system and the right footrest.
7. Detach the starter motor cable from the solenoid switch.
8. Remove the right dust shield and the right engine cover.
9. Release the clutch cable from the arm on the inside of the cover.
10. Break the chain at the connecting link.
11. Disconnect the wiring at the snap connectors.
12. Remove the right plug cap and air-vent tube.
13. Detach the remaining carburettor flange nut.
14. Remove the upper engine mounting bolt from the cylinder head mounting point.
15. Remove the last engine mounting bolt at the rear, and drop the engine from the frame.

Engine Removal: Models CB.72 and CB.77

1. Detach the dual seat by removing the two rear mounting bolts and sliding the seat from its front mounting.
2. Remove the rear mounting bolt from the fuel tank. Detach the fuel pipes.
3. Detach the left footrest and gear-change assembly.
4. Remove the left exhaust system.
5. Release the crankcase well-cover.
6. Free the rev-counter cable from the drive on the cylinder head.
7. Take off the air filter cover and disconnect the battery.

8. Free the startermotor cable from the solenoid.
9. Detach air filter hoses and the throttle cables.
10. Loosen all engine mounting bolts by releasing the nuts.
11. On the right side, detach the brake pedal, footrest, and stop light switch.
12. Detach the right exhaust system.
13. Remove the dynamo cover and the right crankcase cover.
14. Disconnect the clutch cable at the cover end and take off the drive chain connecting link.
15. Disconnect the engine wiring at the snap connectors.
16. Remove the upper mounting bolt, followed by the rear mounting bolts, and drop the engine out of the frame.

Head Removal: Models C.92 and CB.92

1. Remove the contact-breaker cover and disconnect the green wire from the terminal on the plate.
2. Detach the left crankcase cover. If the recess-headed screws are difficult to undo, jar the threads by a sharp blow from a hammer applied to a soft-metal drift placed on the screw heads. Be careful when jarring threads on screws which have no supporting metal around them.
3. Remove the left-hand-threaded 8 mm bolt holding the auto-advance mechanism. Use a hammer to tap the spanner *anti-clockwise*.
4. Remove the alternator rotor. An extractor is required for this. It is possible, however, to utilize the rear-wheel spindle for this job. After the rotor has been removed take out the Woodruff key from the shaft.
5. Remove the four 6 mm bolts holding the starter motor to the front of the crankcase and the two clamps holding the starter cable under the crankcase. That done, twist the motor's sprocket end towards the alternator to free it from its chain. Alternatively, merely remove the starter sprocket circlip and leave the motor in place.
6. Detach the ignition coil from the right side of the crankcase (applicable only to engines up to No. C.92 E-937064).
7. Remove the five cross-headed screws which secure the alternator base plate. This can then be withdrawn, complete with starter chain and sprocket. If the alternative method of removing only the circlip was adopted in step 5 the motor sprocket will come away with the chain.
8. Remove the cam chain tensioner pivot bolt and detach the arm. This is made easier if the cam chain tensioner adjustment screw on the crankcase is first screwed fully home.
9. Rotate the crankshaft until the cam chain link comes to the point where the tensioner's rubber roller previously rested. Remove the link to break the chain.
10. Remove the six cylinder head cover nuts and slide the head from its studs.

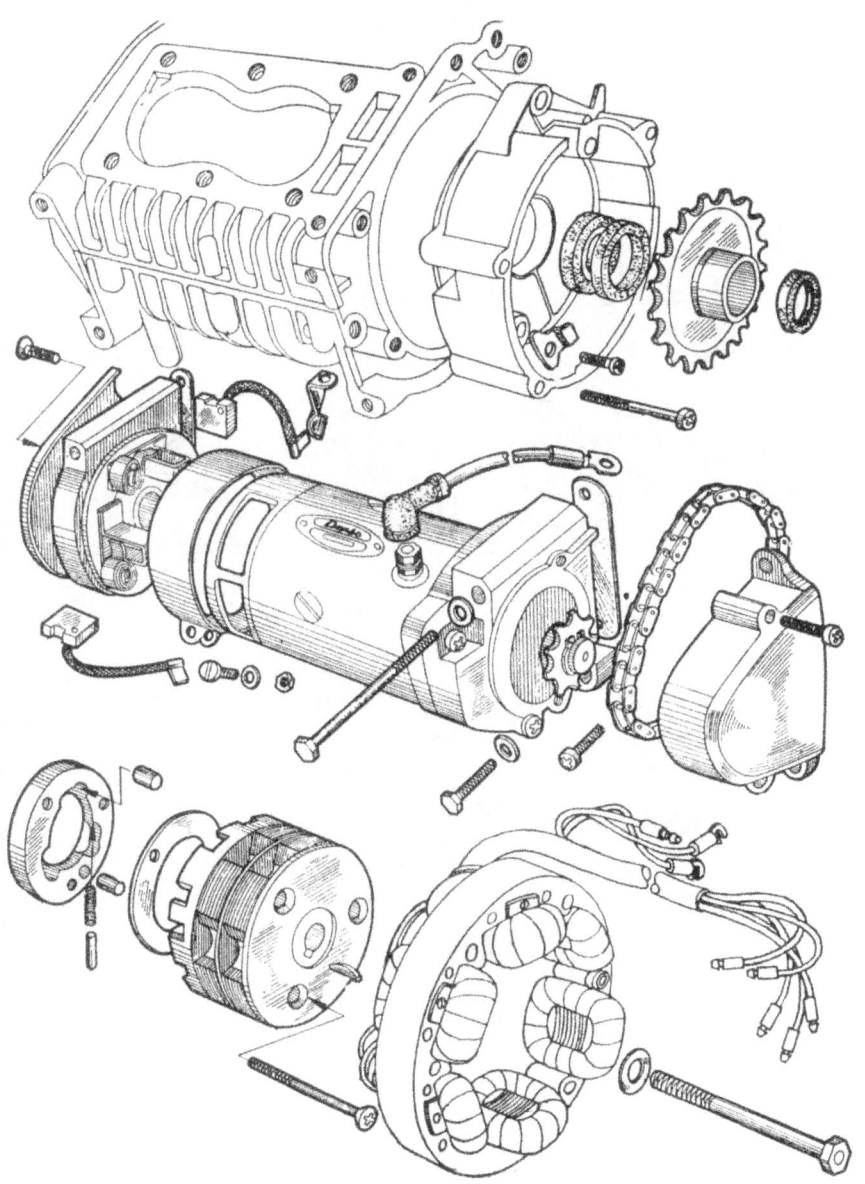

Fig. 39. Starter Motor and Alternator

Here is the layout of the starter motor and the alternator on the C.92 and the CB.92 125 c.c. twin-cylinder models.

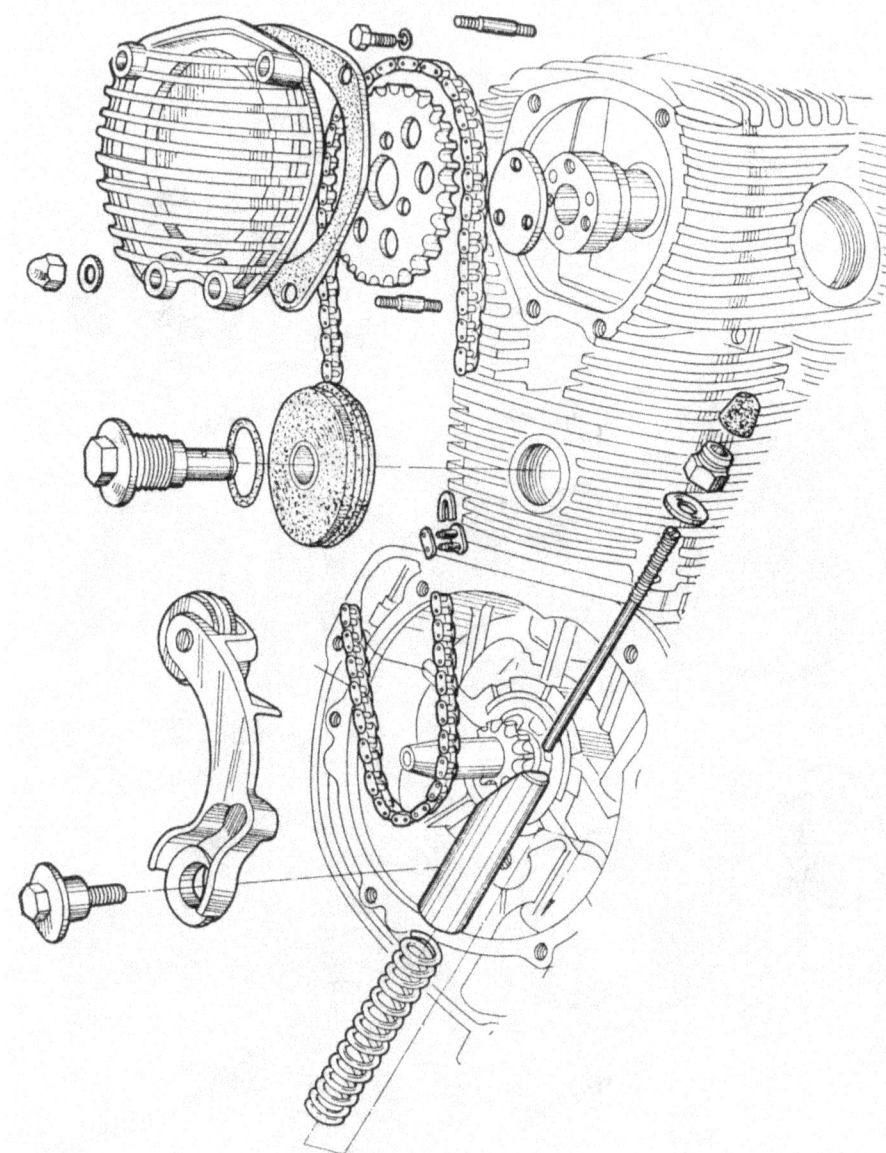

Fig. 40. Overhead Camshaft Drive

An exploded view of the chain drive and tensioner used on both the 125 c.c. twin-cylinder Honda models.

Removal of Valve Gear: Models C.92 and CB.92

1. Detach the left side cover on the head and turn the cam sprocket until the chain is free.
2. Unscrew the three securing bolts and detach the sprocket.
3. Loosen all tappet adjusting screws.
4. On early engines the head carries a distributor. Remove this. On later engines take off the right cylinder head cover.
5. Remove the circlips which locate the rocker shafts.
6. Drive out the rocker shafts using a soft-metal drift.
7. Pull out the camshaft from the drive side opening.
8. Using a valve spring compressor remove the valves. Number them for identification.
9. Decarbonize in the normal way.

Replacing Head and Retiming

1. Reverse the stripping procedure to reassemble the head components. Use a new gasket and a little jointing compound to make an oil-tight joint at the right cylinder head cover plate. When re-installing the camshaft sprocket, note that the bolt hole nearest the timing mark on the sprocket is offset. Therefore, the holes must be accurately aligned before inserting the bolts.
2. Replace the chain, and rotate the sprocket until the inlet side of the chain is six inches longer than the exhaust side.
3. Refit the head. For the purposes of identification the head nuts are considered to be numbered. They are identified as follows (looking at the engine from the rear, as it would be seen by a normally-seated rider): front, left to right, Nos. 5, 1, 3. Rear, left to right, Nos. 4, 2, 6. Of these, No. 6 is a domed nut which must be sealed with a little jointing compound.

Tighten all nuts to finger tightness first. Then lock them up a few threads at a time in the same order as their numbers. If a torque wrench is available it is best to use it. The correct torque for the nuts is 10 ft. lb. minimum and 15 ft. lb. maximum.

4. To time the engine set the "O" mark on the camshaft sprocket alongside the notch cut on the cylinder head. Then turn the crankshaft sprocket so that its timing mark is right at the bottom, but on an extension of a line passing through the two cam sprockets. Join the cam chain at a point adjacent to the crankshaft sprocket, making sure that the spring link is replaced with the open end facing the crankshaft sprocket.
5. Replace the cam chain tensioner, turn the crankshaft slightly in the direction of normal rotation, and loosen the adjuster bolt until the tensioner guide separates from the bolt's lower end. Then tighten the adjuster lock nut, and complete the reassembly of the lower half.

Head Removal: Models C.72, C.77, CB.72, and CB.77

1. Detach the condenser, followed by the eight cylinder head nuts.
2. Remove the cam chain tensioner from the rear of the cylinder block and take out the sparking plugs.

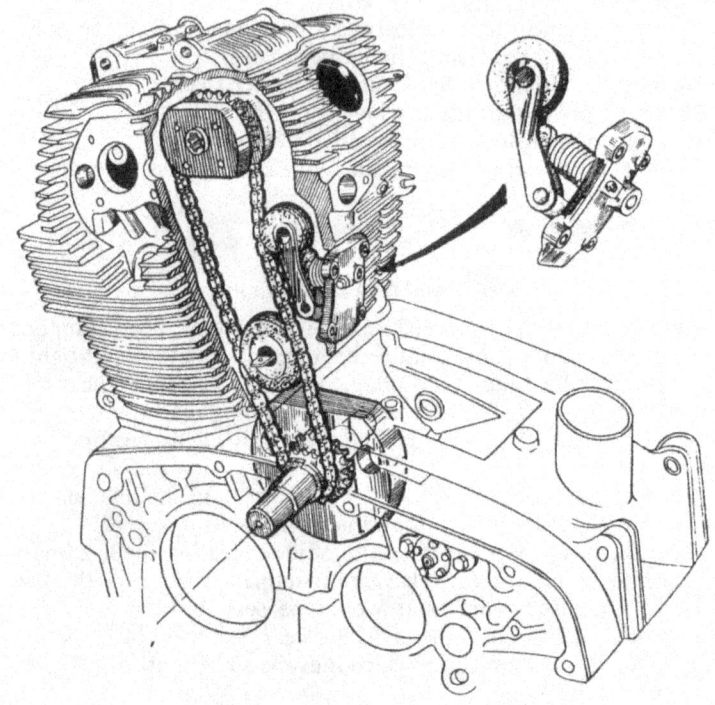

FIG. 41. CAM CHAIN TENSIONER, 250 MODELS

On the 250 c.c. machines—and on the 305 c.c. derivants—this is how the tensioner is arranged. In these machines, the cam chain operates in a tunnel cast into the block and head between the two working cylinders.

3. Turn the crankshaft until the cam chain connecting link is at the top of the camshaft sprocket, projecting through the cylinder head. Remove the link. Take care not to drop it into the tunnel. It is also advisable to loop wire through each free end of the chain to secure it.
4. Lift the cylinder head from its studs.

Removal of Valve Gear: Models C.72, C.77, CB.72, CB.77

1. Remove the valve caps, the contact breaker assembly, and the left cylinder head cover.
2. Loosen all tappet-adjusting screws.

3. Swing each rocker in turn out of the way and insert a Honda valve compressor tool. Compress the spring and, using thin-nosed pliers, lift out the collets. As each valve is removed mark it to ensure that it is refitted correctly, in its original place.

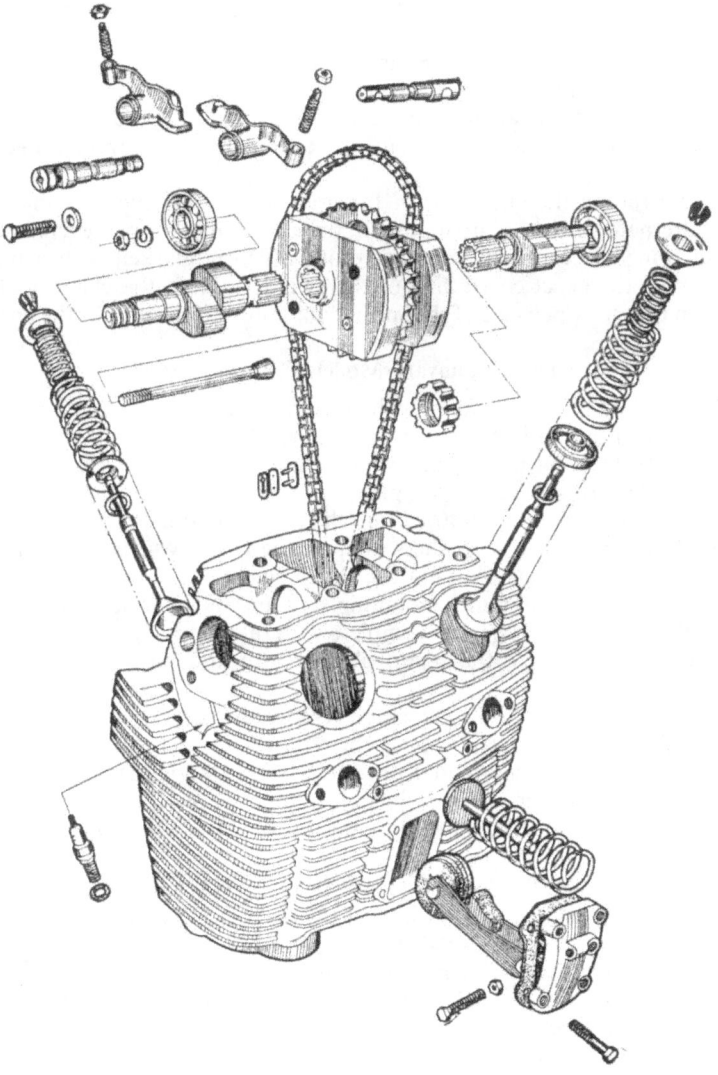

Fig. 42. Valve Gear, 250 and 305 Models
How the valve gear is arranged on the bigger Honda twin motor-cycles.

Replacing Head and Retiming: Models C.72, C.77, CB.72, and CB.77

1. Reinsert all valves.
2. Slide the cylinder head on to its studs and, with the aid of the securing wires, feed the cam chain through the head tunnel and round the sprocket.
3. Refit the head nuts. For the purposes of identification these can be thought of as being numbered in this way, as seen from the saddle: front, left to right, Nos. 6, 2, 4, 8. Rear, left to right, Nos. 7, 3, 1, 5. Of these, Nos. 1, 2, 3, 4 are white nuts and Nos. 5, 6, 7, 8 are tinged yellow. Screw all nuts finger tight at first. Then lock them fully home, two or three threads at a time, working from nut to nut in the correct numerical sequence.
4. To retime the engine, turn the crankshaft until the "T" mark on the alternator rotor is in line with the arrow mark on the crankcase. Then bring the camshaft sprocket tooth which is marked with a punch dot on to the exact centre line of the cylinder. Refit the chain, making certain that the open end of the spring link points to the *rear* of the engine.

Clutch Removal: Models C.92 and CB.92

1. Remove the eleven screws which secure the right crankcase cover.
2. Detach the oil filter cage from the end of the crankshaft.
3. Undo the four 6 mm bolts which retain the clutch centre plate, and remove the springs and friction plates.
4. Pull out the thrust button from the clutch centre.
5. With a pair of circlip pliers, remove the circlip which is set into the end of the main shaft. Pull out the clutch centre.
6. Take out the oil pump mounting stud and its securing bolt.
7. Pull out the clutch body complete with oil pump; remove the thrust washers, and separate the pump plunger arm and piston from the oil pump body.
8. To free the arm from the clutch remove the securing circlip.
9. Take off the left crankcase cover, remove the 6 mm bolt holding the clutch adjuster and detach it from the cover. Unhook the clutch lever spring from the cover.
10. Unscrew the clutch-operating quickthread from the adjuster.

Clutch Reassembly: Models C.92 and CB.92

1. Fit the 20 mm thrust washer on to the transmission shaft, position the oil pump gasket and install the assembled clutch body and oil pump as a unit. Then fit the clutch centre and secure with its circlip.
2. Insert the clutch plates, starting with the single B-type plate. Follow this with, alternately, a friction plate and a plain A-type plate. There are four friction plates and three "A" plates.
3. Insert the pushrod and thrust button. Add the clutch springs and the pressure plate and tighten down with the four 6 mm bolts.

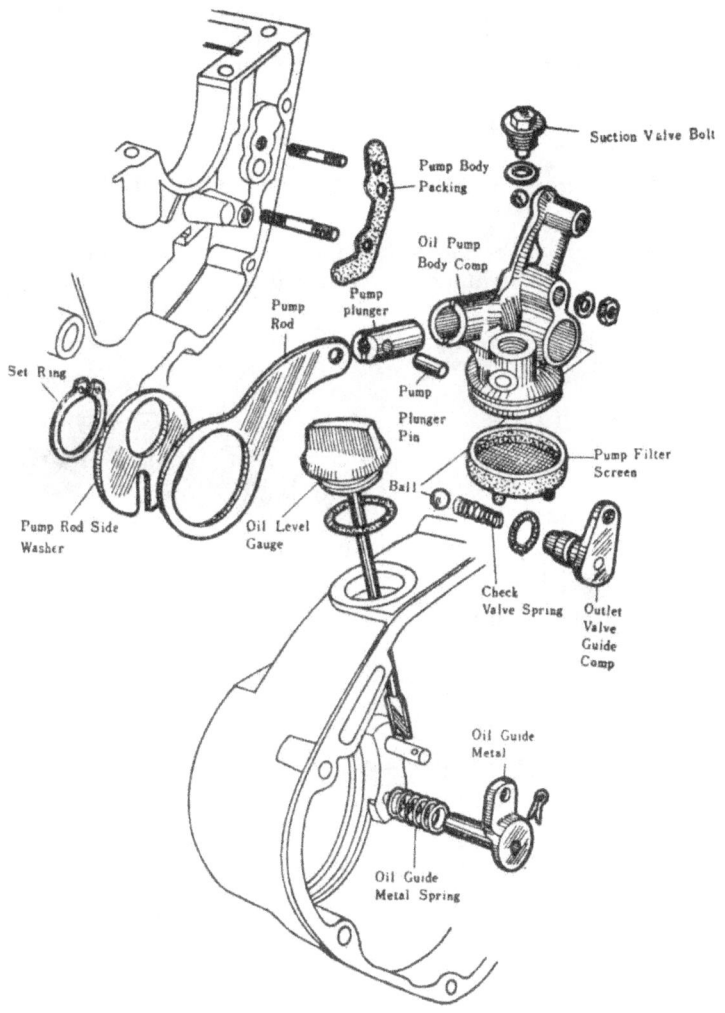

FIG. 43. OIL PUMP ON 125 C.C. TWINS

Operation of the oil pump by an eccentric on the clutch body is an unconventional feature of the 125 c.c. twin-cylinder machines.

4. Refit the oil filter and replace the right crankcase cover.
5. Reassemble the adjuster and quickthread into the left-hand case. Refit the quickthread return spring. Replace the casing.
6. Give several shots of grease through the nipple feeding the operating mechanism.
7. Test and readjust the clutch.

Clutch Removal: Models C.72, C.77, CB.72, and CB.77

1. Remove the left crankcase cover and detach the oil filter and drive.
2. Free the tab washer and remove the crankshaft centre nut.
3. Detach the four 10 mm bolts on the clutch pressure plate.

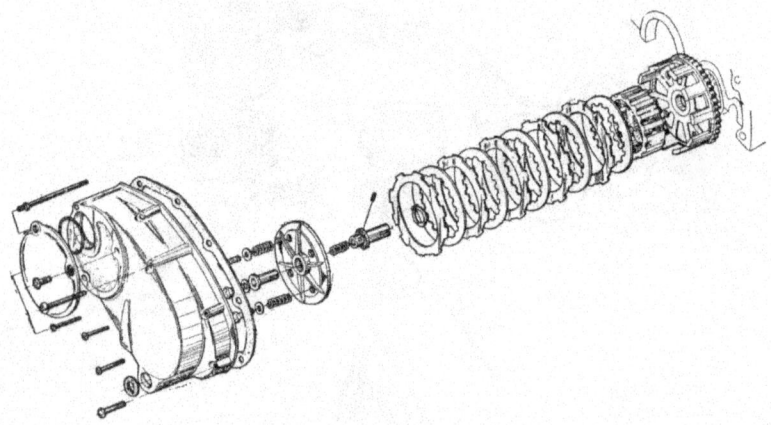

FIG. 44. CLUTCH, CB.72 AND CB.77 TWINS

An exploded view of the clutch on the powerful 250 and 305 c.c. sports twin Hondas.

4. Remove the thrust button.
5. With circlip pliers spring out the 25 mm circlip on the main shaft.
6. Lift out the clutch plates and the clutch centre. Note the order of the plates for subsequent reassembly.

Clutch Reassembly: Models C.72, C.77, CB.72, and CB.77. Merely reverse the above order. When doing so, however, check the operation of the spring-loaded oil conduit. On installation of the clutch pressure plate, tighten the bolts a few threads at a time, working diagonally from one bolt to the next.

Use a new tab washer on the crankshaft sprocket, and when installing the crankcase cover be careful that it does not foul the pin on the oil filter shaft.

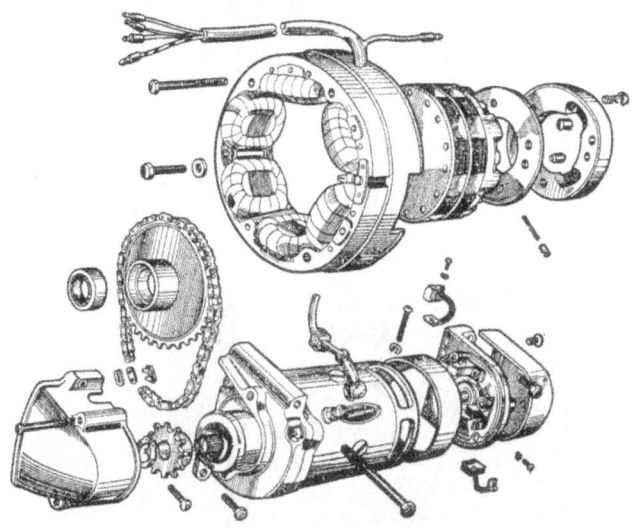

FIG. 45. 250 AND 305 C.C. TWIN "ELECTRICS"
This is the layout of the starter motor and alternator employed on the standard and sports machines in the 250/305 c.c. ranges.

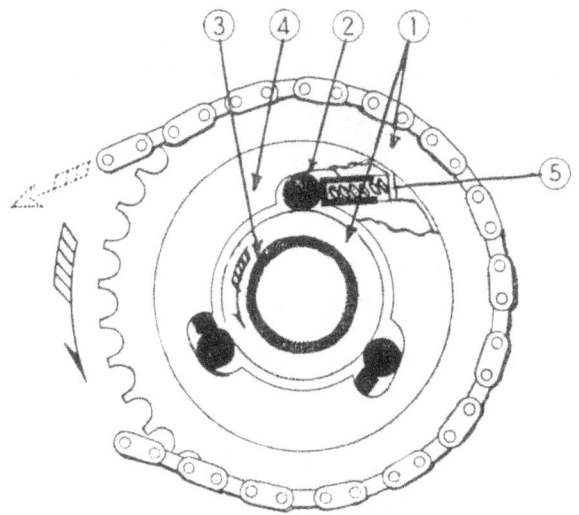

FIG. 46. STARTER MOTOR CLUTCH
This freewheel prevents the starter motor being driven by the engine. When the driven sprocket (1) is rotated in the direction shown by the arrow the rollers (2) are forced against the crankshaft and so turn it. But as soon as the shaft is rotating faster than the drive sprocket centrifugal force throws the rollers outwards in their guides (4) against the resistance of springs (5).

86 THE BOOK OF THE HONDA

Starter Motors. Starter motors are something of an unknown quantity to motor-cyclists. In fact, owing to the comparatively short periods of

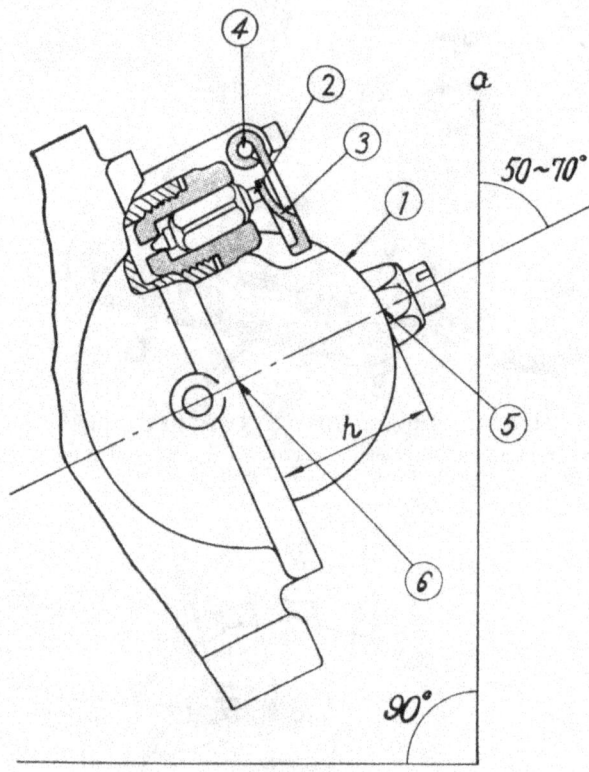

FIG. 47. FUEL LEVEL ADJUSTMENT

On all models except the C.100 and C.102 check the petrol level by removing the float chamber, inverting the carburettor, and tilting it at 50/70 degrees. The distance between the body base and the outer periphery of the float should then be 19·5 mm, plus or minus 0·5 mm (C.110/C.114); between the top of the float and the end of the main jet 7/8 mm (C.92/CB.92); 22·5 mm between the body and outer periphery (PW 26 carburettor) or 26·5 mm (PW 22 carburettor) on the bigger models in the range.

use they require very little attention. To keep them in good order, however, it is advisable to check the brushes and commutator, and to grease the gear casing, every 6,000 miles.

The brushes are set under a removable cover on the starter motor body. Detach this (with the motor on the bench) and loosen the two bolts holding the brush carrier plate. The brushes are held by springs. Check that they are not unduly worn, and that the segments of the commutator

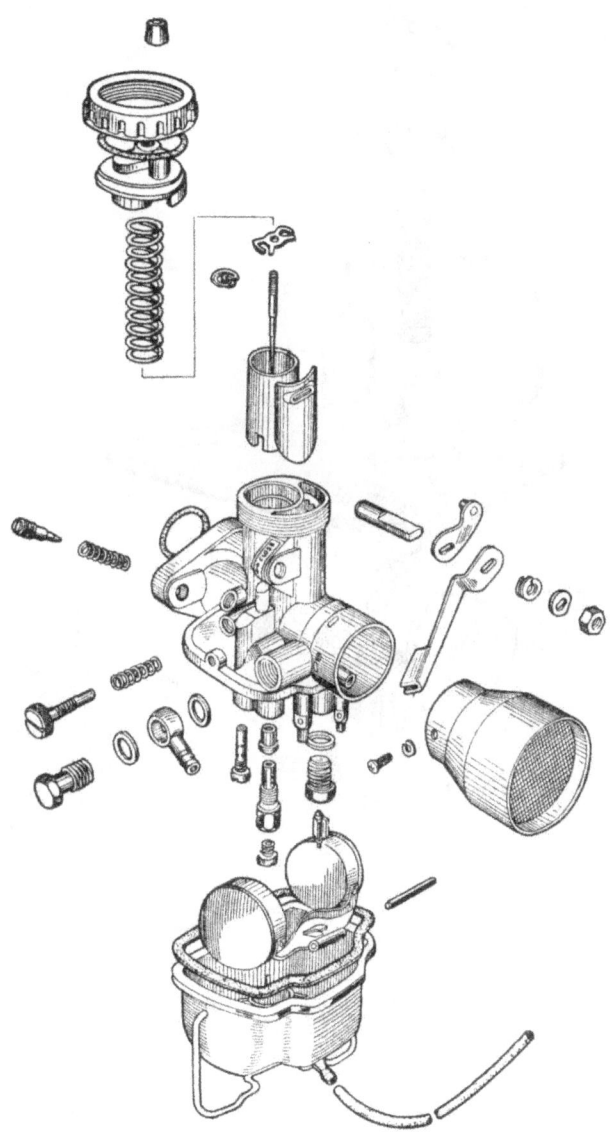

Fig. 48. Carburettor, C.92 Twin

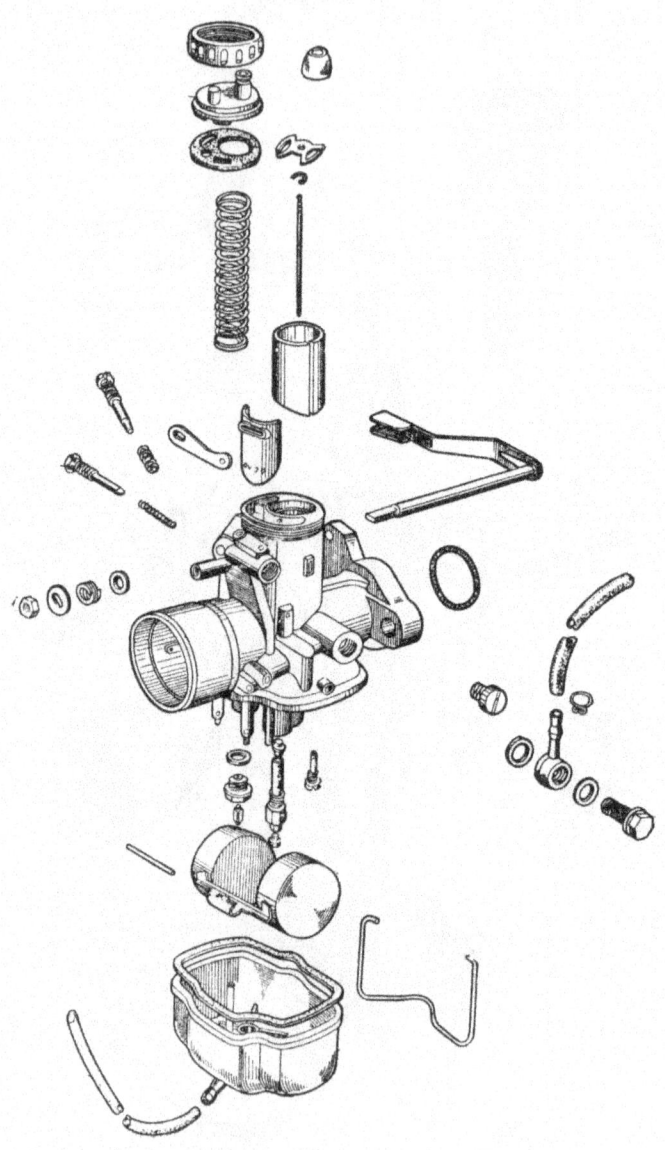

Fig. 49. Carburettor, C.72 Twin

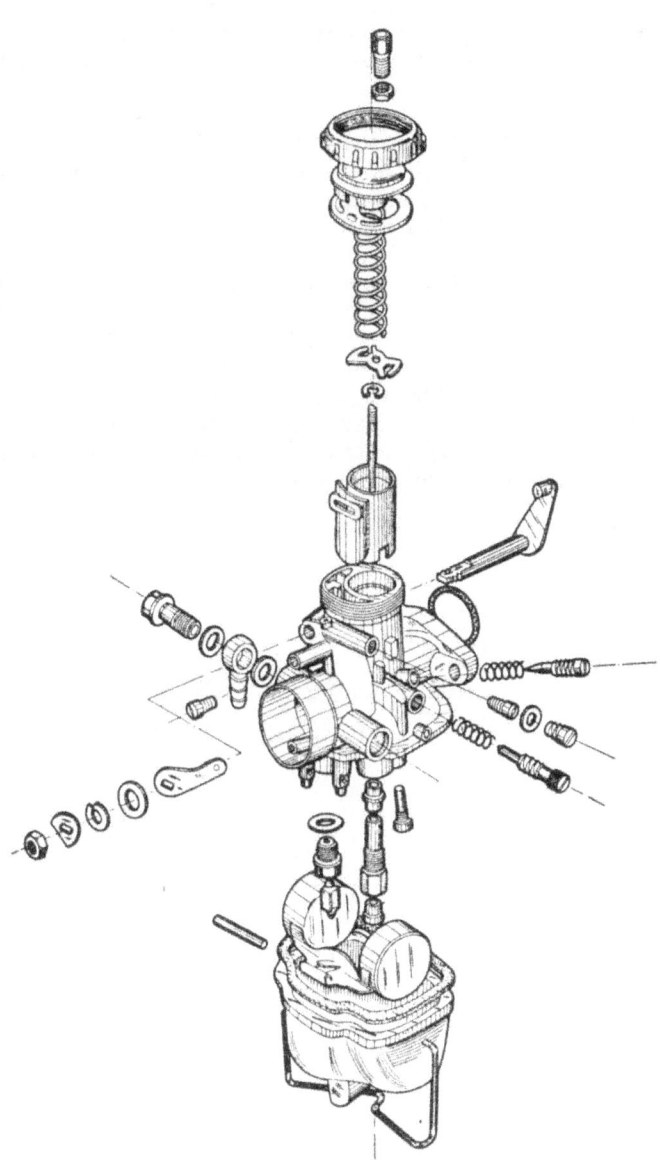

Fig. 50. Carburettor, CB.72 Twin

are not flush with the mica. If they are the mica must be cut back. This *can* be done with a section of broken hacksaw blade, but it is a job best left to an electrical workshop.

Overrunning Clutch. The screech of the Honda's electric-starter overrunning clutch soon becomes familiar to owners. It is normal, and need not therefore be a cause for alarm. This clutch is a sturdy mechanism and it is inadvisable to disturb it.

Rear Chain: Models CB.72 and CB.77. In the absence of a shock absorber, rear chains on these models tend to require frequent adjustment as a result of chain stretch. This can be minimized, I have found, by giving regular attention to chain lubrication.

Every 500 miles, lubricate the chain with Brush-on Linklyfe. This ensures that the drive does not run dry. At intervals of 2,000 miles I have found it advisable to detach the chain and wash it in petrol, following this with an immersion in solid Linklyfe melted over an electric or gas ring.

CHAPTER X

ACCESSORIES FOR HONDAS

So far as the Honda range is concerned the accessories firms have been in for a fairly lean time, these machines featuring as standard equipment many items which would rank as extras on most of their competitors. However, there are one or two items which can be added with advantage.

On the C.100 and C.102 models a windscreen makes a decided difference to the model's utility by improving the weather protection. Some riders tend to question the wisdom of fitting a screen to a machine powered by an engine of only 50 c.c., believing that it will impose an additional strain on the engine by increasing the head resistance. This, of course, is a fallacy, for if there is no screen the head resistance is caused by the rider instead. A screen normally has no greater cross-sectional area than has the human body, but it has a considerably better contour and, if anything, the resulting airflow pattern is an improvement.

My own Honda C.100 has been equipped with a screen embodying a glass fibre handlebar muff. Thus equipped it recorded a running time of just under one hour for 25 miles on a filthy night, heading straight into the teeth of a 40 m.p.h.-plus head wind and climbing the South Downs into the bargain. And this with the engine still stiff, for the machine had then covered only 60 miles all told. The protection offered under those conditions was, to say the least, welcome.

Suitable screens are made by Lambfab and by Stratford, amongst others. The Lambfab is the most expensive. It has a number of refinements including a built-in glove compartment in the muff and provision for the front winking indicators. The necessary extension wiring is provided with the screen, and fitting is quite straightforward. The winkers are detached from the handlebars and the headlamp is removed. The winker wires are then detached at their snap connectors and the extensions slipped into place and led to the lamps, now repositioned on the fibreglass muff. An earthing wire from each lamp goes to the base of the fixing brackets. These are inbuilt and are designed so that the screen unit is held in place by the twin handlebar mirrors.

Other screens are simpler, some being simply Perspex blades fitted to the handlebars by clamps. Since the whole blade is transparent the winkers can be seen through it. Such screens break the force of the wind, keep the rider considerably warmer, and keep off about 80 per cent of the rain and spray which would otherwise land in your lap. Equipped with a screen and with the normal front shielding my C.100 can be ridden for fifty miles or so on a wet day without more than a few splashes reaching unprotected shoes. And for hand protection an ordinary pair of leather walking-out gloves of cuff length normally suffices. Without the screen motor-cycle riding kit is required.

Though screens can also be fitted to the twins most riders prefer to use a specially-designed "dolphin" fairing which offers reasonable weather protection with somewhat better frontal penetration. Such fairings are also produced for the C.110 and C.114 motor-cycles. Prices range from around £12 up to twice that figure, and in some cases it may be better to have the fitting done professionally. One snag is that where such a fairing is fitted to the CB.72 and CB.77 models it becomes impossible to use their forward-acting kick starters, and in winter this may impose an undue load on the battery through constant use of the starter motor.

A rear carrier is a worthwhile investment for any of the machines, since it enables parcels and spare riding kit to be carried with relative ease. Wistonia, G.B.R., and Lambfab make suitable sets designed to bolt on to existing points on the machine—usually the dual seat and suspension anchorages.

My C.100 has a sturdy Wistonia carrier which, used with a pair of aero-elastic straps, gives enough carrying space for a heavy shopping basket.

For twins, the Lambfab carrier is part of a tailored set which includes permanently fixed glass-fibre panniers. These are slung one on each side of the machine and are equipped with forward-hinged lids and locks at the rear. Considerable carrying space is thus available, though with the slight disadvantage that the panniers cannot themselves be used as suitcases. Some of the more expensive types of pannier can in fact be utilized in this way.

When fitting carriers or pannier sets it is extremely important to ensure absolute rigidity. Tighten up all nuts carefully and be certain to use washers whenever these are specified. This is particularly the case with panniers, since these may carry quite heavy loads—and they are mounted well to the rear. Looseness here could have a decidedly deleterious effect on the machine's handling.

Besides screens, fairings, and luggage-carrying equipment a few extra-performance items are also marketed—mainly for the sports 250s and 305s. There are some very special (but expensive) American valve springs which will raise the rev limits to over 10,000 r.p.m., and a close-ratio gear cluster which makes the gearing far more suitable for British road conditions. For the 125 and 250 c.c. sports models there is also a choice of rear sprockets and chains to permit the existing gearing to be varied, so that, for example, a more advantageous top gear can be gained—albeit at the expense of lowering the remaining three ratios.

CHAPTER XI

FUN FROM YOUR HONDA

WHETHER your Honda is a C.100 or a road-burning CB.77 it is something more than just a means of getting from A to B and back again. This is no mere hack, but a machine which is a perennial source of fascination to its rider, and one which is capable of tackling any trip no matter how ambitious.

Continental touring, for example, is well within the bounds of the C.100. For this sort of work it is best to equip the machine with a windscreen—and, of course, a good carrier or pannier set is essential. That apart, all you need in the way of equipment is a G.B. plate and, formalities complied with, the roads of Europe are yours from Mentone to Moscow.

The formalities are simple enough. If you are a member of the A.A. or R.A.C. they will provide all the necessary documents for you. If you are not, my advice would be to join and let the professionals handle it. For one thing these organizations can offer considerable help in the event of an accident or the somewhat unlikelier event of a breakdown abroad. And their fee is ridiculously small—around 70s. for the whole service.

You will need to obtain a Green Card (International Motor Insurance Card) from your insurers and an extra premium will certainly be asked, since most motor-cycle insurances do not automatically cover foreign touring. They will need to know the engine and frame numbers and the registration number, the dates of your trip, and the countries you intend to visit. It is as well to allow yourself a few days' grace in case there is some unexpected delay on the journey.

One point here is that the normal insurance may not cover your riding kit and personal effects. Many companies will arrange the necessary extra cover for a small premium.

To enable you to "export" your Honda temporarily you will require a Customs Form 29 C (Sale), which is available free from Customs and Excise offices. If the A.A. or R.A.C. are handling your arrangements they will provide this for you. It is a two-part form on which are entered the details of your machine. When you leave Britain the Customs authorities retain one part, and sign the other. This signed duplicate enables you to bring your machine back into the country without payment of purchase tax or duty.

Should you be buying your machine on hire purchase, a word of warning is apposite. You are *not* the owner of the machine, but only the hirer. Therefore, you have no right to "export" the machine; nor even to sign the declaration form as its owner. To take your mount overseas you will need to have the written permission of its true owner, the finance company. Providing your account with the company is in good standing this permission is unlikely to be withheld, but to avoid any possible disappointment you should ask for permission, in writing, at least a month or six weeks before your contemplated trip abroad.

For most countries, these documents—plus the registration book or a photostat copy of it—will suffice, though for Eastern Europe a Carnet is also needed. This is a largish book containing tear-out sheets, each of which covers entry or exit from one particular country.

Your personal document will be a passport or a British Visitor's Passport. The full passport is valid for five years, costs thirty shillings, and can be obtained from the Passport Office, Petty France, London S.W.1, or from employment exchanges. The visitor's passport is valid for a year, costs seven and six, and can be had from any office of the Ministry of Labour.

Some countries still require visas—documents permitting you to enter and leave the country—and application for this must be made well in advance to the appropriate Embassy. In some countries it is necessary to have an International Driving Licence (valid for one year).

For camping it is advisable to obtain an International Camping Carnet. This can be issued by the motoring organizations or by the caravanning bodies. It permits you to use sites maintained by international camping clubs affiliated to British ones and may sometimes carry with it a reduction in fees.

Money for touring is best taken in the form of travellers' cheques. You pay a small commission on these, but the added security is well worth it. And in some cases it is possible to obtain petrol concession coupons in Britain which can be exchanged abroad for petrol at a very advantageous rate. Indeed, in the case of some East European countries the saving is in the region of fifty or seventy-five per cent of the domestic cost.

Getting abroad is a very painless procedure financially for the owner of a Honda. On the air ferries, for example, a C.100 can be conveyed from Britain to France for as little as half a crown! Thus the cost of a return air fare to France for machine and rider could be under £7; and the time taken from arrival at the airport to driving away on the other side of the Channel can be as little as half an hour. Oddly enough, it is more expensive by sea—at least so far as the machine is concerned—though the passenger fare is less. From Dover to Calais, return, would work out to roughly £5, but the time involved in the crossing is about an hour and a half and formalities take considerably longer by virtue of the fact that a ship carries far more vehicles and passengers than does an aircraft.

What can be expected of a Honda as a touring mount? Fully laden, a C.100 is capable of covering between twenty-five and thirty miles in an hour quite comfortably. Supposing that one rides from nine in the morning till one and from two until six, or equivalent hours, a daily mileage of between 200 and 250 miles would not be impossible. For example, by use of the Channel air ferry one could ride to Rome in five days, spend five days there, and ride home again all within the space of a fortnight's holiday. And the transport costs for such an expedition should amount only to £14 or so, including the Channel crossing in both directions.

With a CB.72 the costs are obviously higher, but long-distance pillion work becomes a practical proposition—and 350 miles or more can be covered each day on the fast Continental roads. With such a potential, even the Middle East can come into your reckonings—especially if you give yourself literally the benefit of a flying start by using one of the long-distance air-ferry services.

For example, two people on a CB.72 could cross the Channel by air for a total return cost of about £17. Five days' riding could see them 1,750 miles away—and the cost of fuel for such a return journey would still be only £12. So for a total outlay on transport of under £30 they could enjoy a ride to the Levant and back and spend nearly a week there out of a fortnight's holiday. With more money to spend use of the air ferry direct to Geneva would extend their touring range by about 600 miles. The return cost would be approximately £81 for two people on a CB.72; or £35 for one rider with a C.100.

You may also care to weigh the advantages of Scandinavia as a touring ground. One shipping company, operating from Newcastle, will carry vehicles free of charge when they are accompanied. Not, of course, that you have to go abroad to get fun from your Honda. With its constant changes of scenery and local speech and customs, Britain is an ideal touring ground. And given 200 miles motoring each day, it is almost possible to ride right round the coast of Britain in a fortnight—a project for which a Honda is admirably suited. A word of warning here, however: always carry a spare can of petrol strapped to the carrier, for even today it is possible to cover many miles and not find a petrol pump open—especially in the more remote parts of Scotland or Wales.

So much for holidays by Honda. But weekends can also be turned to good account by using your machine for day or weekend trips. And even the smallest Honda is quick enough to make it possible for you to join your local motor-cycle or scooter club and take part in their weekend runs and main-road competitive events. There is much to be said for club life. Not only does it add to your circle of friends, but also it enables you to learn from the experiences of others—and those experiences are very freely exchanged on club nights!

You can obtain the name and address of the secretary of your local club or the Honda Owners' Club, catering specially for Honda enthusiasts, from the A.-C.U., 83 Pall Mall, London S.W.1. A national one-make club, the Honda Owners' Club has branches in various parts of the country.

Perhaps you feel that you would like to put your Honda to use for social purposes in the wider sphere? In that case you might care to become a member of the Volunteer Emergency Service. This was founded during a smallpox scare a few years ago, when two great motor-cycling enthusiasts, Barry and Margaret Ryerson, realized that volunteer motor-cycle despatch riders could distribute urgently-needed vaccines faster than could any of the official services. From that idea has grown a wonderful stand-by corps of riders willing to be on call to help others—a truly magnificent answer to the widespread and ill-informed criticism which the motor-cycle and scooter community have had to bear. The address is: 1 Plough Lane, Wallington, Surrey.

For work, play, or social service I am sure you will find that your Honda will give you untold pleasure. I know for certain that my personal Hondas have done so, and that they will continue to do so. You have an engineering masterpiece which, given the necessary minimum of attention, will never let you down. And if this book gives you a little more insight into the working of your machine and helps you care for it a little better, then I will feel amply repaid in the knowledge that there is yet another fellow rider who is enjoying trouble-free motor-cycling on a Honda.

APPENDIX
FACTS AND FIGURES

APPENDIX

FACTS AND FIGURES

Data	C.100	C.102	C.110	C.114
Bore . . .	40 mm	40 mm	40 mm	40 mm
Stroke . .	39 mm	39 mm	39 mm	39 mm
Capacity . .	49 c.c.	49 c.c.	49 c.c.	49 c.c.
C.R. . . .	8·5:1	8·5:1	9·5:1	9·5:1
Output . .	4·5 b.h.p. at 9,500 r.p.m.	4·5 b.h.p. at 9,500 r.p.m.	5 b.h.p. at 9,500 r.p.m.	5 b.h.p. at 9,500 r.p.m.
Ignition timing (full advance) .	35° b.t.d.c.	35° b.t.d.c. (Stable)	35° b.t.d.c.	35° b.t.d.c.
Ring gap (compression) . .	0·003/0·010 in.	0·003/0·010 in.	0·003/0·010 in.	0·003/0·010 in.
Ring gap (oil control rings) .	0·003/0·010 in.	0·003/0·010 in.	0·003/0·010 in.	0·003/0·010 in.
Exhaust valve length . . Inlet valve length	60·6–60·8 mm (2·3858–2·3937 in.) 61·1–61·3 mm (2·4055–2·4134 in.)			
Valve spring free length (outer) .	27 mm (1·063 in.)		28·4 mm (1·118 in.)	
Valve spring free length (inner) .	27·8 mm (1·0945 in.)		26·9 mm (1·0591 in.)	
Pushrod length (inlet) . .	187·4 mm (7·3779 in.)			
Pushrod length (exhaust) . .	170·5 mm (6·7126 in.)			
Contact breaker gap . . Sparking plug gap	0·014 in. 0·024 in.	0·014 in. 0·024 in.	0·014 in. 0·024 in.	0·014 in. 0·024 in.
Tappet clearances	0·002–0·004 in. cold			
Main jet . .	88/95	88/95	85/88	85/88
Slow running jets	35	35	35	35
Throttle slide .	2	2	2 (Pw 16)	2 (Pw 16)

C.92	CB.92	C.72	CB.72/77*
44 mm	44 mm	54 mm	54/60 mm*
41 mm	41 mm	54 mm	54 mm
124 c.c.	124 c.c.	247 c.c.	247/305 c.c.*
8·3:1	10:1	8·3:1	9·3:1
11·5 b.h.p. at	15 b.h.p. at	20 b.h.p. at	24/28½* b.h.p. at
9,500 r.p.m.	10,500 r.p.m.	8,000 r.p.m.	9,000 r.p.m.
40° b.t.d.c.	40° b.t.d.c.	40° b.t.d.c.	45° b.t.d.c.
0·0059/0·014 in.	0·0059/0·014 in.	0·0059/0·014 in.	0·0059/0·013 in.
			0·008/0·016 in.*
0·0059/0·014 in.	0·0059/0·014 in.	0·0039/0·012 in.	0·0039/0·012 in.
57·1–57·3 mm	88·65–88·85 mm	88·74–88·76 mm
58–58·2 mm	89·18–89·38 mm	89·96–89·98 mm
1·137 in.	1·725 in.	1·707 in.
1·189 in.	1·364 in.	1·477 in.
Not applicable
Not applicable
0·012/0·020 in.	0·012/0·016 in.	0·012/0·016 in.
0·024/0·028 in.	0·027 in.	0·027 in. (standard);
		0·015 in. (racing)
0·004 in. cold
90	85	115	100/135*
40	35	35	35/42*
Pw 18/520	Pw 18/2·5	Pw 22; Hov/520	3/2*

Data	C.100	C.102	C.110	C.114
Jet needle	13302	13302	16302	16302
Turns out, air screw adjuster	1/1¼	1/1¼	1/1¼	1/1¼
Oil capacity	1⅛ pints	1⅛ pints	1⅛ pints	1⅛ pints
Oil grade (winter)	20 S.A.E.	20 S.A.E.	20 S.A.E.	20 S.A.E.
(summer)	30 S.A.E.	30 S.A.E.	30 S.A.E.	30 S.A.E.
Petrol tank capacity	6·4 pints	6·4 pints	1·6 gal.	1·6 gal.
Sparking plug	Type N.G.K. C7 HW (10 mm × 12·7 mm reach) or K.L.G. T90 (10 mm)			
Tyre pressure:				
front	22 p.s.i.	22 p.s.i.	22 p.s.i.	22 p.s.i.
rear	28 p.s.i.	28 p.s.i.	28 p.s.i.	28 p.s.i.
rear (pillion)	32 p.s.i.	32 p.s.i.	32 p.s.i.	32 p.s.i.
Bulbs:				
head	6 V 15/15 W	6 V 20/20 W	6 V 15/15 W	6 V 15/15 W
tail	6 V 1·8 W	6 V 1·8 W	6 V 1·8 W	6 V 1·8 W
stop	6 V 6 W	6 V 6 W	6 V 6 W	6 V 6 W
winker	6 V 8 W	6 V 8 W	6 V 8 W	6 V 8 W
neutral	6 V 3 W	6 V 3 W	6 V 3 W	6 V 3 W
	small bayonet	small bayonet	small bayonet	small bayonet
winker indicator	—	—	,,	,,
speedo	6 V 1·5 W	6 V 1·5 W	6 V 1·5 W	6 V 1·5 W
Weight (dry)	143 lb.	154 lb.	145 lb.	146 lb.
Length	71·25 in.	71·25 in.	67 in.	67 in.
Width	22·25 in.	22·25 in.	22·24 in.	22·24 in.
Height	37·25 in.	37·25 in.	36·25 in.	36·25 in.
Ground clearance	5½ in.	5½ in.	5·9 in.	5·9 in.
Tyre sizes	2·25 × 17 in. front and rear			

* Denotes data applicable to 305 c.c. Model CB.77 only.

FACTS AND FIGURES

C.92	CB.92	C.72	CB.72/77*
Pw 18/24	Pw 18/24	Pw 22; Hov 24	22402/24231*
1/1½	1/1½	1/1½	1½/1¼*
2·1 pints 20 S.A.E. 30 S.A.E.		2·7 pints 20 S.A.E. 30 S.A.E.	
2·4 gal	2·8 gal	2·6 gal	3 gal
C7H or C10H (10 mm × 12·7 mm reach)		C7HW (10 mm)	C7HW or C10H
1964 onwards: D9H (D8H during running in); D10 or D11; K.L.G. TW220 (TW100, town use). All 12 mm.			
25 p.s.i. 30 p.s.i. 40 p.s.i.		21 p.s.i. 28 p.s.i. 40 p.s.i.	24 p.s.i. 31 p.s.i.
6 V 30/20 W 6 V 3 W 6 V 6 W 6 V 8 W 6 V 2 W		12 V 35/35 W 12 V 4 W 12 V 8 W 12 V 10 W 12 V 3 W	12 V 35/30 W 12 V 4 W 12 V 7·5 W
6 V 3 W		12 V 3 W	12 V 3 W
264 lb 76 in. 25½ in. 37·4 in. 5·12 in.	242 lb 73½ in. 23½ in. 36·4 in. 5½ in.	356 lb 78·4 in. 27·6 in. 37·4 in. 5½ in.	336/350* lb 79·7 in. 24·2 in. 39·4 in. 5·12 in.
3·00 × 16 in. front and rear	2·50 × 18 in. front 2·75 × 18 in. rear	3·25 × 16 in. front and rear	2·75 × 18 in. front 3·00 × 18 in. rear

INDEX

A.C. GENERATOR, 77
Accessories, 91–2
Air filter, 21, 60
Automatic clutch, 5, 25, 54, 55

BATTERY, 63
Benley, C.92, 1, 74–90
Benley, CB.92, 2, 74–90
Big end, 9
Brakes, 7, 25, 26, 44, 45
   adjustment, etc., 61, 62
Bulbs, 63, 100, 101

CAMSHAFT, 14, 72
Carburettor, 19, 20, 21, 28, 56, 57, 58, 59, 64, 87–9
Chain. *See* transmission
Clutch, 5, 23, 24, 32, 72, 82, 84
   adjustments, 54, 55
Compression ratio, 31
Connecting rod, 9
Contact breaker, 18, 30, 52
Crankcase, 9, 72
Crank pin, 9
Cylinder, 9, 67, 71, 82
C.100, C.102, CE.105H, 1, 50–73
C.110, C.114, 1, 50–73

DAILY maintenance, 45–6
Decarbonizing, 64–82
Direction indicators, 100, 101
Dream (C.72, CB.72, C.77, CB.77), 2, 74–90

ELECTRICAL circuits, 32, 40
Engine overhaul, 74–90
   principles, 9–21

FAULT tracing, 27
Flywheel magneto, 19
Flywheels, 9
Four-stroke cycle, 11
Front forks, 25
Fuel tank, 100, 101
   troubles, 27, 28

GEARBOX, 6, 22
Gudgeon pin, 9, 10

HANDLEBAR assembly, 4
Headlamp, 100, 101
Hydraulic dampers, 25

IGNITION—
   coil, 17
   faults, 29, 30
   leads (H.T.), 29, 30
   principles, 16, 17
   timing, 98, 99

JETS, 20, 57, 58, 59

KICK starter, 4

LUBRICATION, 14, 15, 16, 47

MAINTENANCE—
   daily, 46
   routine, 44, 47
   weekly, 46

OIL filters, 48, 49
   pump, 14, 16, 83
Oils, etc., 32, 47
Overhead camshaft, 78, 80

PETROL filters, 28
   tap, 4, 28, 55, 60
Piston, 9, 67, 70
Piston rings, 9, 68
Pushrods, 13, 98

R.A.C./A.-C.U. Training Scheme, 3
Rockers, 13, 81

SILENCER, 61
Sparking plugs, 12, 29, 51, 100–1
Specifications, 98–101
Starter motor, 77, 85, 86, 90
Suspension, front 25
   rear, 25

THROTTLE slide, 20
Timing—
  ignition, 53
  valves, 73
Tools, 41–3
Transmission, 22, 63, 90
Twist grip, 4
Tyre pressures, 100, 101
Tyres, 100, 101

VALVE, 9, 31, 45, 68, 69, 79, 80, 82
  grinding, 68
  guides, 45
  springs, 14, 70
  tappets, 14, 30, 50

WIRING diagrams, 33, 34, 35, 36, 37, 38, 39
  faults, 29, 30, 32, 40

OTHER BOOKS CURRENTLY AVAILABLE FROM

www.VelocePress.com

AUTOBOOKS SERIES OF WORKSHOP MANUALS

ALFA ROMEO GIULIA 1750, 2000 1962-1978 WORKSHOP MANUAL
AUSTIN HEALEY SPRITE, MG MIDGET 1958-1980 WORKSHOP MANUAL
BMW 1600 1966-1973 WORKSHOP MANUAL
FIAT 124 1966-1974 WORKSHOP MANUAL
FIAT 124 SPORT 1966-1975 WORKSHOP MANUAL
FIAT 500 1957-1973 WORKSHOP MANUAL
FIAT 850 1964-1972 WORKSHOP MANUAL
JAGUAR E-TYPE 1961-1972 WORKSHOP MANUAL
JAGUAR MK 1, 2 1955-1969 WORKSHOP MANUAL
JAGUAR S TYPE, 420 1963-1968 WORKSHOP MANUAL
JAGUAR XK 120, 140, 150 MK 7, 8, 9 1948-1961 WORKSHOP MANUAL
LAND ROVER 1, 2 1948-1961 WORKSHOP MANUAL
MERCEDES-BENZ 190 1959-1968 WORKSHOP MANUAL
MERCEDES-BENZ 230 1963-1968 WORKSHOP MANUAL
MERCEDES-BENZ 250 1968-1972 WORKSHOP MANUAL
MG MIDGET TA-TF 1936-1955 WORKSHOP MANUAL
MINI 1959-1980 WORKSHOP MANUAL
MORRIS MINOR 1952-1971 WORKSHOP MANUAL
PEUGEOT 404 1960-1975 WORKSHOP MANUAL
PORSCHE 911 1964-1969 WORKSHOP MANUAL
RENAULT 8, 10, 1100 1962-1971 WORKSHOP MANUAL
RENAULT 16 1965-1979 WORKSHOP MANUAL
ROVER 3500, 3500S 1968-1976 WORKSHOP MANUAL
SUNBEAM RAPIER, ALPINE 1955-1965 WORKSHOP MANUAL
TRIUMPH SPITFIRE, GT6, VITESSE 1962-1968 WORKSHOP MANUAL
TRIUMPH TR2, TR3, TR3A 1952-1962 WORKSHOP MANUAL
TRIUMPH TR4, TR4A 1961-1967 WORKSHOP MANUAL
VOLKSWAGEN BEETLE 1968-1977 WORKSHOP MANUAL

OTHER WORKSHOP MANUALS, MAINTENANCE & TECHNICAL TITLES

AUSTIN HEALEY SIX CYLINDER CARS 1956-1968
BMW ISETTA FACTORY REPAIR MANUAL
FERRARI 250/GT SERVICE AND MAINTENANCE
FERRARI GUIDE TO PERFORMANCE
FERRARI OPERATING, MAINTENANCE & SERVICE HANDBOOKS 1948-1963
FERRARI OWNER'S HANDBOOK
FERRARI TUNING TIPS & MAINTENANCE TECHNIQUES
MASERATI OWNER'S HANDBOOK
OBERT'S FIAT GUIDE
PERFORMANCE TUNING THE SUNBEAM TIGER
PORSCHE 356 SERVICE AND MAINTENANCE MANUAL 1948-1965
PORSCHE 912 WORKSHOP MANUAL
VOLVO ALL MODELS 1944-1968 WORKSHOP MANUAL

MOTORCYCLE WORKSHOP MANUALS, MAINTENANCE & TECHNICAL TITLES

ARIEL MOTORCYCLES WORKSHOP MANUAL 1933-1951
BMW MOTORCYCLES FACTORY WORKSHOP MANUAL R26 R27 (1956-1967)
BMW MOTORCYCLES FACTORY WORKSHOP MANUAL R50 R50S R60 R69S R50US R60US R69US (1955-1969)
HONDA MOTORCYCLES FACTORY WORKSHOP MANUAL 250cc TO 305cc C/CS/CB 72 & 77 SERIES 1960-1969
HONDA MOTORCYCLES MAINTENANCE AND REPAIR 50cc TO 305cc C100, C102, MONKEY BIKE, CE 105H TRIALS BIKE, C110, C114, C92, CB92, BENLEY, C72, CB72, C77 & CB77
NORTON MOTORCYCLES FACTORY WORKSHOP MANUAL 1957-1970
NORTON MOTORCYCLES WORKSHOP MANUAL 1932-1939
TRIUMPH MOTORCYCLES FACTORY WORKSHOP MANUAL NO. 11 (1945-1955)
TRIUMPH MOTORCYCLES WORKSHOP MANUAL 1935-1939
TRIUMPH MOTORCYCLES WORKSHOP MANUAL 1937-1951
VINCENT MOTORCYCLES MAINTENANCE AND REPAIR 1935-1955

CLASSIC AUTO TITLES & REFERENCE BOOKS

ABARTH BUYERS GUIDE
DIALED IN ~ THE JAN OPPERMAN STORY
FERRARI 308 SERIES BUYER'S AND OWNER'S GUIDE
FERRARI BERLINETTA LUSSO
FERRARI BROCHURES & SALES LITERATURE 1946-1967
FERRARI SERIAL NUMBERS PART I ~ STREET CARS TO SERIAL # 21399 (1948-1977)
FERRARI SERIAL NUMBERS PART II ~ RACE CARS TO SERIAL # 1050 (1948-1973)
FERRARI SPYDER CALIFORNIA
IF HEMINGWAY HAD WRITTEN A RACING NOVEL ~ THE BEST OF MOTOR RACING FICTION 1950-2000
LE MANS 24 ~ WHAT THE MOVIE COULD HAVE BEEN
MASERATI BROCHURES AND SALES LITERATURE ~ POSTWAR THROUGH INLINE 6 CYLINDER CARS

CHECK OUR WEBSITE AT

www.VelocePress.com

OR CONTACT YOUR DEALER FOR PRICING

www.ingramcontent.com/pod-product-compliance
Lightning Source LLC
Chambersburg PA
CBHW070558170426
43201CB00012B/1874